Restorative Justice

David A. Schultz and Christina DeJong
General Editors

Vol. 5

PETER LANG
New York • Washington, D.C./Baltimore • Bern
Frankfurt am Main • Berlin • Brussels • Vienna • Oxford

Ruth Ann Strickland

Restorative Justice

PETER LANG
New York • Washington, D.C./Baltimore • Bern
Frankfurt am Main • Berlin • Brussels • Vienna • Oxford

Library of Congress Cataloging-in-Publication Data

Strickland, Ruth Ann.
Restorative justice / Ruth Ann Strickland.
p. cm. — (Studies in crime and punishment; v. 5)
Includes bibliographical references and index.
1. Restorative justice. 2. Victims of crimes. 3. Criminals—Rehabilitation.
4. Corrections—Philosophy. 5. Criminal justice, Administration of.
I. Title. II. Series.
HV8688.S78   345'.001—dc21   2003006800
ISBN 0-8204-5758-2
ISSN 1529-2444

Bibliographic information published by **Die Deutsche Bibliothek**.
Die Deutsche Bibliothek lists this publication in the "Deutsche
Nationalbibliografie"; detailed bibliographic data is available
on the Internet at http://dnb.ddb.de/.

Cover design by Dutton & Sherman Design

© 2004 Peter Lang Publishing, Inc., New York
275 Seventh Avenue, 28th Floor, New York, NY 10001
www.peterlangusa.com

All rights reserved.
Reprint or reproduction, even partially, in all forms such as microfilm,
xerography, microfiche, microcard, and offset strictly prohibited.

Contents

Chapter 1: Restorative Justice   1
    Definition of the Restorative Justice Alternative   1
    Historical Origins of the Restorative
        Justice Movement   2
    Uses of Restorative Justice   4
    Restorative Justice: General Practices   5
    Restorative Justice: Specific Techniques   9
    Preview of Upcoming Chapters   14

Chapter 2: Restorative Justice and Defendants   19
    Restoring Communities, Victims, and Defendants   19
    Taking Responsibility Versus Legal Guilt   21
    Widening the Net of Social Control   24
    Reintegrating and Restoring Offenders   24
    Reduction in Offender Recidivism   26
    Defendants and Legal Rights   28

Proportionality in Punishment 30
Restorative Justice and Dangerous Defendants 32
Conclusions 34

Chapter 3: Restorative Justice and Victims 37
Victim Services 39
Victim-Offender Panels 40
Family Group Conferencing 42
Victim-Offender Reconciliation and Mediation 45
Victim Compensation and Restitution 48
Healing and Sentencing Circles 51
Victim Impact Statements 53
Reparative Boards 56
Conclusions 58

Chapter 4: Restorative Justice and
the Courtroom Workgroup 62
Police 63
Prosecutors 66
Defense Attorneys 70
Judges 74
Conclusions 82

Chapter 5: Restorative Justice and the Community 86
Defining Community 86
Community Justice and Crime 88
Communities of Interest and Responsibility 89
Community Involvement in Restorative Justice 90
Diverting Criminal Cases to Community Groups 93
Community Empowerment 95
Community Partnerships with Criminal
    Justice Agencies 97
Community Restoration 104
Building Community Support for Restorative Justice 105

Chapter 6: Restorative Justice and Corrections 110
Restorative Justice and the Multiple
    Goals of Corrections 110
Traditional Community-Based Corrections 111
Restorative Justice and Community-Based
    Corrections 112
Traditional Community-Based Corrections
    Revamped with a Restorative Focus 113

CONTENTS   vii

>   Restorative Justice Techniques with
>   Correctional Implications   121
>   Implications of Restorative Justice for Corrections   130

Chapter 7: Conclusions   137
>   Implications of Restorative Justice   141
>   The Future of Restorative Justice   141

CHAPTER 1

Restorative Justice

Definition of the Restorative Justice Alternative

Restorative justice, a term first used in the late 1970s, describes a series of processes designed to repair the harm that a criminal offense inflicts on victims, offenders, and communities (Braithwaite 1999, 1743). A relatively new movement in the fields of victimology and criminology, restorative justice requires the parties with a stake in a particular crime—the victims, offenders, and communities—to work together to repair the harm of crime and prevent future harm. Because crime causes injuries to everyone involved, restorative justice advocates insist that all affected parties participate in a restorative process (Restorative Justice Online, Tutorial: Introduction to Restorative Justice). This process places emphasis on restoring the emotional and material losses of victims, providing forums for dialogue among stakeholders, and sponsoring negotiation and problem solving in the community. The aim is to promote greater community safety and more harmonious relationships (Office of Justice Programs, "Working Definitions of Restorative Justice").

According to Kurki (2000, 265), restorative justice is different from current mainstream criminal justice practice. First, it does not focus solely on crime as a lawbreaking event. It looks at crime in a broader context and examines the harm crime inflicts on victims, communities, and offenders. Second, it empowers more people. More parties are involved in redressing the crime—not just governmental officials and the offender. Victims and communities play a role. Third, it measures success based on how well harm is repaired or prevented rather than how many offenders are incarcerated and convicted. It stresses the victims' and the communities' needs and focuses less on the guilt of offenders, the danger they represent, or their criminal histories.

Historical Origins of the Restorative Justice Movement

Restorative justice is not a new concept and has been present in justice systems throughout history. John Braithwaite, a scholar and prominent advocate of restorative justice practices, believes that restorative justice has been the leading model of justice for most of the world's people throughout human history in both Western and non-Western traditions.

Retributive justice—harsh sentencing and punitive criminal law—is actually a recent development in Western history. This model dates back only a few centuries. Restorative justice—sometimes referred to as community justice—dates back much further in history. In the past, communities were deemed the most important source of social control. The harm inflicted on communities through crime was viewed as best reconciled by community dispute resolution processes (Llewellyn and Howse 2002).

Howard Zehr (2002, 3) attributes the recent interest in restorative justice to some of the limitations associated with the traditional Western legal system practices. The limitations are based on the perception that the reliance on harsh sentencing practices does not reduce recidivism rates and that punitive criminal law does not adequately redress the harms inflicted on society and victims by offenders. Neither harsh sentencing nor punitive criminal law promotes peace and healing of victims, communities, or offenders. According to Zehr (2003, 4), these perceived limitations promoted consideration of restorative justice practices. Since the 1970s, numerous programs have emerged in many countries, including the United States, the United Kingdom, Australia, Canada, South Africa, and New Zealand. Throughout the world, thousands of communities are offering restorative justice practices alongside the traditional, more retributive criminal justice system.

Restorative justice theory owes much to movements that sought to address failures and inequities in the traditional criminal justice system. Van Ness and Strong (1997, 16–20) identify these movements as: the informal justice movement, the movement to use restitution as a response to crime, the victim's rights movement, the reconciliation and conferencing movement and the social justice movement. Here is a brief description of these movements:

1. The *informal justice movement* emphasized the need for alternative dispute resolution and increased community/layperson access to the legal system. This movement shifted more responsibility to communities for resolving conflict and attempted to reduce stigmatization of offenders and the use of coercion.
2. The *movement to use restitution as a response to crime* in the 1960s focused attention on the needs of victim and in some cases, community restitution as well.

3. The *victim's rights movement* made a case for inclusion of victims in the legal process and recognition that without victim participation, the justice system would crumble.
4. The *reconciliation and conferencing movement* introduced two major components associated with restorative justice: victim-offender mediation and family group conferencing. These processes drew on traditions in non-Western cultures to give communities a voice in reconciliation and repairing the harm associated with crime.
5. The *social justice movement* is an umbrella descriptor of a variety of groups working together for a vision of social justice that did not coincide with retributive justice.

Van Ness and Strong (1997, 9) point out that numerous pre-colonial African societies used compensatory sanctions rather than punitive ones. Confession, repentance, and seeking absolution have been prominent parts of Japan's justice system throughout history. Ancient cultures, such as the aboriginal peoples and Native American tribal societies, used restorative justice practices that emphasized mending relationships, repairing harm to the community, and addressing the underlying causes of conflict.

Uses of Restorative Justice

Citizen Empowerment: Based on community participation, restorative justice has potential as an empowerment tool. Its most basic framework involves the participation of all stakeholders—victims, offenders, key supporters of victims, key supporters of offenders, and community members (Pranis n.d.). Consequently, it has the capacity to empower community members by involving them directly in the administration of justice. It redefines crime as an affront to victims and the community rather than the state.

Local Control Enhances Citizen Understanding and Satisfaction: It provides for local control over the administration of justice.

The incorporation of citizen input and advice is essential. Citizen education about the operations and functions of criminal justice agencies enhances citizen understanding of the criminal justice process. Potentially, increased citizen interaction with criminal justice agencies will also increase their satisfaction with the services these agencies provide.

Crime Prevention: With citizen awareness raised and with greater citizen participation, more crime prevention may occur. Instead of focusing on crime after it happens, restorative justice places a strong emphasis on identifying the root causes of crime and stopping crime before it happens. Through building communities and providing neighborhood sponsored skill based programs and early intervention programs, restorative justice advocates believe crime prevention is more likely (Kurki 2000, 237–238).

Restorative Justice: General Practices

Restorative justice encompasses a wide array of practices and techniques. Advocates do not suggest one single plan of action but rather rely on local communities to identify practices that work best for them. Generally, practices associated with restorative justice in the United States include community crime prevention, community policing, community prosecution, problem-solving courts, and community corrections. These practices are not always explicitly linked to restorative justice. These general practices share some but not all philosophical tenets of the restorative justice movement.

Community Crime Prevention and Community Justice

Restorative justice advocates believe that crime is a social problem that undermines the quality of life in communities. This core belief guides the prescription and requires a new role and mode of operation of criminal justice agencies

(Kurki 2000, 236–237). Part of the solution is community-oriented crime prevention.

Community crime prevention programs address the root causes of community conflicts by keeping conflicts from escalating into crimes. Although governments must provide order, communities are responsible for creating cohesion and peace. Restorative justice advocates argue that peace, unlike order, can not be imposed and must be fostered through cooperative ventures between community residents and criminal justice agencies (Bright, "Community Crime Prevention," 1997).

Community justice is an effort to establish partnerships between local government agencies, the private sector and the community to promote community peace. It fosters a holistic approach to public safety by linking the community to police, courts, corrections and victim concerns, and defining community as a social network for problem solving (Office of Justice Programs, "Definitions of Community Justice").

Community Policing

Community policing sponsors the development of closer ties to the community. This enables law enforcement officials to better serve the community's needs. It consists of a partnership between the police and the community. This partnership is aimed at reducing the fear of crime and the crime rate and improving the quality of life in the target community.

In theory, community policing includes everyone in the community—residents, city administrators and employees, educators and school officials, and church members. All citizens assume responsibility for the community's well being. There are many routes to community policing and it encompasses a wide array of programs such as foot and bike patrols, Drug Abuse Resistance Education (DARE), senior check-ups, citizen police academies, juvenile diversion, family crisis intervention, midnight basketball, and initiatives that portray officers as friendly in elementary schools (Brown 2001, 55–58). Citizen-police partnerships allow the police and the communities they serve to work together on issues of concern and to reach shared solutions (Nicholl 1999, 23-24).

Community Prosecution

Touted as community policing's legal partner, community prosecution requires prosecutors to invite citizen participation in setting crime-fighting priorities and in establishing collaborative relationships that are beneficial to prosecutors and community residents. Community prosecution requires prosecutor sensitivity to the needs of community residents' concerns and a long-term commitment of resources for implementing community-based programs. Traditional methods of priority-setting in prosecutor offices focuses on the seriousness of the crime, the sufficiency of evidence, and the threat that defendants pose to others or themselves. Community prosecution, on the other hand, most often addresses less serious crimes, such as loitering or prostitution, that threaten a community's quality of life. Looking beyond the traditional role as case processor, prosecutors use community prosecution to give citizens a stake and some responsibility for promoting public safety (Weinstein 1998). Community prosecution could lead to more input from victims and make them feel more like partners in the process (Forst 2000, 141).

Problem-Solving Courts and Therapeutic Jurisprudence

Problem-solving courts are on the rise in the United States (Brienza 1999). They consist of specialized drug courts, domestic violence courts, community courts, mental health courts, and numerous others. Many problem-solving courts are linked to therapeutic jurisprudence. Therapeutic jurisprudence seeks to individualize justice by looking at the individual needs of each offender and seeking a therapeutic option—one that promotes health and healing but does not conflict with legal norms (Rottman and Casey 2000).

The community courts technique fosters collaboration between a trial court and one or more community groups. The citizenry consult with the court in a major aspect of its adjudication responsibilities (Villa 1996). Problem-solving courts, which include community courts, encourage lawyers, who typically operate in the adversarial mode in the United States, to help change offenders' behavior patterns and to protect community well-being. Feinblatt and Denckla (2001, 207) maintain that traditional adjudication does not deal well with complex problems such as drug addition, domestic violence, and mental illness.

The purpose of both community-focused courts and problem-solving courts is to promote better court practices, better public access, and increased public knowledge of the courts. These courts take many different forms. The types and varieties of community courts and problem-solving courts will be discussed in more detail in chapter 4.

Community-Based Corrections

A variety of community corrections options are incorporated into restorative justice. Examples of more recent developments in community corrections include restitution, community service, intensive supervision, home confinement and electronic monitoring, out-patient treatment, community-based residential settings, employment and education requirements, day-reporting center, and fines (Kleiman 1999). Unlike probation and parole, which also are part of community corrections, the more recent instruments of community corrections are aimed at offender reintegration into society (Branham 1995, 418). Community-based corrections, such as community-based probation centers, offer treatment, education, job-placement services, skill development, and try to create positive changes in offenders' lives through family and community intervention (Kurki 2000, 261).

Two instruments commonly employed in the restorative justice mode are victim restitution and restorative community service. Direct restitution requires offenders to pay victims a sum of money to compensate them for financial losses incurred by the crime. Community service requires offenders repay the community by providing a community benefit. Both instruments are used to redress the harm that crime inflicts on communities. Restorative justice advocates believe judges should be given wider discretion to use community corrections for offenders who pose no significant danger or threat to their communities (Leven 1993, 654–655).

Restorative Justice: Specific Techniques

More specific techniques associated with restorative justice include diversion, victim-offender reconciliation, victim impact panels, victim impact statements, family or community conferencing, community peacemaking or sentencing circles, reintegrative shaming, and prisoner assistance programs.

Diversion

One technique associated with restorative justice is pretrial diversion. When offenders enter pretrial diversion, usually after arrest, they are removed from the traditional court and trial processes and placed into alternative programs. Diversion to alternative programs usually requires offenders to admit guilt and to meet a set of conditions. If offenders meet the conditions, charges are suspended or dismissed. Post-conviction diversion is also possible. A case may be referred to alternative programs even at this point. If an offender meets the conditions associated with a restorative process, the conviction might be set aside or vacated (Van Ness and Nolan 1998, 72–75).

Victim Offender Reconciliation/ Mediation Program

Victim offender mediation allows interested victims to meet with their offenders in a safe setting with the guidance of trained mediators. Mediators facilitate discussion of the crime and provide victims and offenders a chance to work out a plan that alleviates the harm. Offenders are encouraged to learn about the effects of crimes on victims and to assume responsibility for the harms caused (Kurki 2000, 269–270; Umbreit and Greenwood 2000, 7).

The three basic goals of victim-offender reconciliation are to identify the injustice, to set things right, and to examine a future course of action. Victims get an opportunity to meet with offenders and to explain their injuries and losses. Offenders, in turn, have a chance to express remorse and explain their actions (Braswell, et al. 2001).

Victim-Offender Panels

Unlike victim-offender mediation, which sponsors a direct meeting between a victim and an offender, victim-offender panels allow unrelated victims and offenders, linked only by a similar offense, to meet. Victim-offender panels are useful when a victim or an offender refuses to meet the other directly. These panels attempt to promote victim healing and closure. Offenders may begin to understand the extent of damage inflicted on others by their actions (Bright "Victim-Offender Panels," 1997).

Victim and Community Impact Statements

The federal government and all fifty states allow victims and victims' survivors the opportunity to address the sentencing authority, in person or in writing, about the impact of a crime on their lives. In this way, victims explain the physical, psychological, and economic harm suffered due to the crimes perpetrated against them. Often, victims also express their opinions about the type of sentence their offenders should receive. Considered an important expansion of victims' rights, victim impact statements, despite constitutional challenges continue to thrive (Tobolowsky 1999, 71).

In the 1990s, the trend was toward community input in criminal sentencing, not just victim input. In *Payne v. Tennessee* (501 U.S. 808), the U.S. Supreme Court introduced the possibility of community input at criminal sentencing. Organized groups increasingly are involved in criminal sentencing by sending community impact statements to judges which chronicle the damage done by the crime and describe community losses. Some community groups also monitor trials, keeping records of conviction rates and sentences (Long 1995, 199).

Victim and community impact statements are linked to the restorative justice movement's emphasis on victim and community reparation. This movement encourages community and victim ties to the system so that the community accepts some responsibility for controlling criminality and delinquency (Viano 2000).

Family or Community Group Conferencing

According to Umbreit (2002, 2), conferencing, unlike victim-offender mediation, involves a larger number of people. Conferencing allows victims, offenders, and their key supporters to meet and decide how to deal with the aftermath of a crime. A facilitator contacts the victim and offender, inviting them to the conference and describing its purpose. The facilitator then asks them to identify key supporters whom they would like to participate in the conference. Participation is voluntary for all parties. Offenders must take responsibility for their offenses in order to participate. The trained facilitator convenes all the parties and helps them discuss how individuals were harmed by the crime and how that harm might be repaired.

The victim's response to the crime raises the offender's awareness of its impact and offenders have an opportunity to take responsibility for their actions. Supporters of offenders may provide a network of support and may help them make amends. In effect, they take collective responsibility for the offender and try to prevent any future offense. Supporters of the victims provide important social support and may promote a speedier healing process (Umbreit 2002, 2).

Community Peacemaking or Sentencing Circles

Based on traditional Native American practices, sentencing circles attempt to build a consensus among all interested parties on the appropriate sentencing plan for an offender. All parties with a stake in the outcome are involved including victims, offenders, community members, victim supporters, offender supporters, judges, prosecutors, defense counsels, police, and court workers (Sharpe 1998, 39).

Circles assume that responsibility for addressing crime and its impact resides with the community. This means that the individual who commits a crime is not the only one responsible for the criminal event. The family and community who let the offender "lose his way" also share responsibility for restoring the community and helping the victim heal (Sharpe 1998, 39).

Sentencing circles take different forms but share some commonalities. As described by Sharpe (1998, 40), often the process begins either with a prayer or a ceremony that strikes a chord with the participants. Introductions and a statement of purpose start the process. Usually, the offender speaks first and presents a brief summation of the offense. A facilitator—then—promotes a discussion (some circles may leave it to participants to determine how the discussion will unfold).

Sharpe (1998, 40) also notes that many circles simply continue the meeting until everyone has had his or her say. These discussions center on how people were harmed by the specific crime but also allude to similar crimes committed in the past in that community. They attempt to determine the underlying causes of the crime and ways in which the community might prevent future occurrences. Agreements reached by the circles state what must be done to promote healing of the victim, offender, the family, and the community.

Reintegrative Shaming

Reintegrative shaming expresses disapproval of an individual's offensive behavior while also sponsoring activities that allow the offender to re-enter society without feeling like an outcast (Braithwaite1989, 100- 101). Reintegrative shaming uses apology-forgiveness ceremonies as part of victim-offender mediation or reconciliation. Some shaming ceremonies are stigmatizing. Braithwaite (2000) and Braswell, et al. (2001) emphasize that stigmatizing shaming—publicizing an offender's crime without some linkage to forgiveness—actually makes crime worse. Through reintegrative shaming, offenders have an opportunity to earn their way back into communities. At the same time, communities seek ways to reintegrate the redeemed offenders into the community. Whether reintegrative shaming can successfully be employed in a modern, individualistic culture—such as the United States—will be addressed in chapter 6.

Prisoners Assistance Programs

Most prisons train inmates how to be good prisoners, not functional members of a free society. Consequently, restorative justice advocates argue that alternatives to incarceration and community-based sanctions should be used when applicable (Cayley 1998). When these alternatives are not applicable and incarceration is a necessity, they also argue for prisoners assistance programs—programs that help prisoners make a smoother and more productive transition back into society. Various programs—such as Sentencing Concepts Inc. (Sentencing Concepts Inc. "Alternative Sentencing Programs), Habitat for Humanity's Prison Partnership, and Ohio's Offender Services Network—offer reintegration services to prisoners (Sentencing Concepts Inc. "Alternative Sentencing Programs; Ta 2000, 114–115; "Ohio Provides Seamless Transition to the Street Through the Offender Services Network" 1998). Restorative justice advocates argue that community ties are very important to offenders who seek to reintegrate. The approaches used to help offenders transition back into the community will be discussed in greater detail in chapter 6.

Preview of Upcoming Chapters

Chapter 1 defines restorative justice, provides a brief description of its origins and examines some of the restorative justice practices employed in some parts of the United States. The following chapters will provide in-depth discussions on the implementation and effects of restorative justice practices on defendants and offenders, victims, the courtroom workgroup, communities, and corrections in the United States.

Chapter 2 examines the effects of restorative justice practices on defendants and offenders. By examining one the goals of restorative justice—to heal and reintegrate offenders—this chapter provides an overview of how restorative justice practices could improve the plight of defendants and offenders in the United States by reducing the reliance on punitive sanctions. At the same time, the introduction of restorative justice practices may be inhibited by the framework and assumptions of an adversarial process and by a cultural emphasis on individual rights.

Chapter 3 provides an overview of the victims' rights movement and the role of the victim in restorative justice practices. This chapter investigates the workings of as well as the evaluations of victim-offender panels, family group conferencing, victim-offender reconciliation and mediation, victim compensation and restitution, healing and sentencing circles, victim impact statements, and reparative boards.

Chapter 4 gives a detailed examination of how the courtroom workgroup—policy, prosecutors, defense attorneys and judges—could incorporate and in some cases, have incorporated, restorative justice practices in the traditional criminal justice system. The police, for example, may employ community/restorative policing, use citizen police academies and rely on police-based family group conferencing. Prosecutors may control their caseloads more effectively by engaging in pretrial diversion, referring offenders to victim offender reconciliation and incorporating community prosecution. Typically driven by the adversarial model, defense attorneys still may sponsor a more community-oriented approach by use of whole client representation, defense attorney collaboration, defense community outreach, and by adopting a problem-solving orientation. Various judges have also adopted restorative justice practices by relying on the tenets of therapeutic justice and participating in community and problem-solving courts.

Chapter 5 defines the community's relationship to restorative justice. It emphasizes community responsibilities and interests in resolving and repairing the harm inflicted on society by crime. As the community is essential to making restorative justice a reality, this chapter explores the contentions that modern societies lack a real sense of community and therefore are not able to realistically adopt restorative justice practices. This chapter also examines the effects of diverting criminal cases to community groups and how civil libertarians react to this trend. It is also a matter of controversy whether communities are empowered by restorative justice processes and chapter 5 notes the arguments presented by both proponents and opponents. Various community partnerships with criminal justice agencies and community restoration efforts are also examined.

Chapter 6 deals with the effects of restorative justice techniques, such as sentencing circles, reintegrative shaming, and victim-offender reconciliation, on the correctional system. This chapter provides a description of how traditional community-based correctional programs—such as probation and parole, electronic monitoring, work release, restitution, and community service—can be revamped with a restorative justice focus.

Chapter 7 provides a summary of the findings in chapters 1 through 6. It discusses the implications of restorative justice for the traditional criminal justice system and the possibilities of more widespread use of restorative justice techniques.

References

Berman, Greg. 2000. "What Is a Traditional Judge Anyway?—Problem Solving in the State Courts." *Judicature* 84 (September–October): 78–85.

Braithwaite, John. 1989. *Crime, Shame and Reintegration.* Cambridge: Cambridge University Press.

Braithwaite, John. 1999. "A Future Where Punishment Is Marginalized: Realistic or Utopian?" *UCLA Law Review* 46 (August): 1727–1750.

Braithwaite, John. 2000. "Shame and Criminal Justice." *Canadian Journal of Criminology* 42 (July): 281–298.

Branham, Lynn S. 1995. "A Federal Comprehensive Community-Corrections Act: Its Time Has Come." *Thomas M. Cooley Law Review* 12: 399–429.

Braswell, Michael, John Fuller, and Bo Lozoff. 2001. *Corrections, Peacemaking, and Restorative Justice: Transforming Individuals and Institutions.* Cincinnati: Anderson Publishing.

Brienza, Julie. 1999. "Community Courts Reach Out to Put a Dent in Petty Crime." *Trial* 35 (March): 14–16.

Bright, Christopher. 1997. "Community Crime Prevention." < http://www.restorativejustice.org > (accessed May 31, 2001).

Bright, Christopher. 1997. "Victim-Offender Panel." < http://www.restorativejustice.org > (accessed May 31, 2001).

Brown, Jim. 2001. "Community Policing Reality Check." *Law & Order* 49 (April): 55–58.

Cayley, David. 1998. *The Expanding Prison: The Crisis in Crime and Punishment and the Search for Alternatives.* Toronto: House of Anansi Press.

Feinblatt, John, and Derek Denckla. 2001. "Prosecutors, Defenders and Problem-Solving Courts." *Judicature* 84 (January–February): 207–214.

Forst, Brian. 2000. "Prosecutors Discover the Community." *Judicature* 4 (November–December): 135–141.

Kleiman, Mark A. R. 1999. "Community Corrections as the Front Line in Crime Control." *UCLA Law Review* 46: 1909–1925.

Kurki, Leena. 2000. "Restorative and Community Justice in the United States." *Crime and Justice* 27: 235–291.

Leven, David C. 1993. "Curing America's Addiction to Prisons." *Fordham Urban Law Journal* 20 (Spring): 641–657.

Llewellyn, Jennifer J. and Robert Howse. 2002. "Restorative Justice—A Conceptual Framework." < http:www.lcc.gc.ca/en/themes/sr/rj/howse/howse_main.asp > (accessed September 1, 2003).

Long, Katie. 1995. "Community Input at Sentencing: Victim's Right or Victim's Revenge?" *Boston University Law Review* 75 (January): 187–229.

Nicholl, Caroline G. 1999. "Community Policing, Community Justice, and Restorative Justice: Exploring the Links for the Delivery of a Balanced Approach to Public Safety." Washington, D.C.: U.S. Department of Justice, Office of Community Oriented Policing Services.

Office of Justice Programs. "Definitions of Community Justice." < http://www.ojp.usdoj.gov/nij/rest-just/ch1/cjdef1.htm > (accessed May 31, 2001).

Office of Justice Programs. "Working Definitions of Restorative Justice." < http://www.ojp.usdoj.gov/nij/rest-just/ch1/cjdef1.htm > (accessed May 31, 2001).

"Ohio Provides 'Seamless' Transition from Prison to the Street Through the Offender Services Network." 1998. *Alternatives to Incarceration* 4 (November/December): 10.

Pranis, Kay, Restorative Justice Online, n.d. "Building Community Support for Restorative Justice." < http://www.restorativejustice.org > (accessed May 31, 2001).

Restorative Justice Online, n.d. "Tutorial: Introduction to Restorative Justice," < http://www.restorativejustice.org > (accessed May 31, 2001).

Rottman, David, and Pamela Casey. 2000. "Therapeutic Jurisprudence and the Emergence of Problem-Solving Courts." *Alternatives to Incarceration* 6 (Spring): 27–30.

Sentencing Concepts Inc., n.d. "Alternative Sentencing Programs," < http://www.sciconcepts.com/brochure/1_over.htm > (accessed June 7, 2001).

Sharpe, Susan. 1998. *Restorative Justice: A Vision for Healing and Change*. Edmonton: Edmonton Victim Offender Mediation Society.

Ta, Christine. 2000. "Prison Partnership—It's About People." *Corrections Today* 62 (October): 114–115.

Tobolowsky, Peggy M. 1999. "Victim Participation in the Criminal Justice Process: Fifteen Years After the President's Task Force on Victims of Crime." *New England Journal on Criminal and Civil Confinement* 25 (Winter): 21–105.

Umbreit, Mark S. 2000. "Family Group Conferencing: Implications for Crime Victims." Washington, D.C.: U.S. Department of Justice, Office for Victims of Crime.

Umbreit, Mark S., and Jean Greenwood. 2000. "Guidelines for Victim-Sensitive Victim-Offender Mediation: Restorative Justice Through Dialogue." Washington, D.C.: U.S. Department of Justice, Office for Victims of Crime.

Van Ness, Daniel W. and Pat Nolan. 1998. "Legislating For Restorative Justice." *Regent University Law Review* 10: 53–110.

Van Ness. Daniel, and Karen Hertdeeks Strong. 1997. *Restoring Justice*. Cincinnati: Anderson Publishing Company.

Viano, Emillo. 2000. "Restorative Justice for Victims Offenders: A Return to American Traditions." *Corrections Today* 62 (July): 132–135.

Villa, Judy. "Juvenile Justice: Community Courts," *Nevada Policy Research Institute Issue Brief* (January 27, 1996/1997) < http://www.npri.org/issues/issues97/juve_justice.htm > (accessed June 7, 2001).

Weinstein, Susan P. 1998. "Community Prosecution: Community Policing's Legal Partner." *FBI Law Enforcement Bulletin* 67 (4): 19–24.

Zehr, Howard. 2002. *The Little Book of Restorative Justice*. Intercourse, PA: Good Books.

CHAPTER 2

Restorative Justice and Defendants

Restoring Communities, Victims, and Defendants

One of the chief aims of restorative justice is to focus on re-establishing the integrated community, rather than exacting retribution for crimes. Many proponents of restorative justice attribute the failure of today's criminal justice system to its historical reliance on vengeance. From a restorative justice advocate's perspective, crime injures not just the victim, but the community and the offender as well. Defendants, who participate in restorative processes, admit their wrongdoing and thus are automatically classified as offenders. The primary purpose of the criminal justice system, from a restorative point of view, is to repair the harms caused by the offense. For advocates of restorative justice, then, promoting reconciliation and peace between and among the affected parties is more important than vengeance.

Although restorative justice proponents reject the crime control model which emphasizes punishment over reconciliation, they do not necessarily adhere to the due process model, which focuses almost exclusively on the individual rights of criminal defendants, or the rehabilitative model, which seeks to heal offenders but not victims. They assert that these approaches do not deal with the effects of crime on victims, communities, and offenders sufficiently.

To heal and reintegrate offenders, the participation of community actors and victims in a restorative process is explicitly required. Much uncertainty surrounds the implementation of restorative processes in the United States. It is a serious question if victims would be willing to face, and confront, and possibly bargain with someone who inflicted harm on them. Maybe victims would not want to revisit such a traumatic event. Other victims may not be ready to forgive or let go of their resentment. Some offenders may not be able to participate in a meaningful way due to lack of remorse or because of mental illness.

David Neubauer (2002, 390–391) claims that questions remain unanswered as to whether restorative justice programs will be completely integrated into the criminal justice system, operate independently of it or even replace it completely. Some restorative justice advocates are clearly anti-State and would prefer a criminal justice system based on fewer criminal justice professionals and operating on the basis of layperson norms and practices. Still others point out that alternative dispute resolution processes are more likely to succeed if integrated into existing criminal justice agencies.

Kurki (2000, 241) argues that a systemwide shift is desirable if restorative justice is a more humane approach to dealing with crime, if restorative justice initiatives will have only sporadic effects unless channeled through the system systematically, and if restorative justice programs will be marginalized by criminal justice agencies who, seeing them as temporary interlopers, will refuse to divert offenders to them.

The answers to these questions—whether significant numbers of victims can be encouraged to participate in restorative justice processes and whether restorative justice processes are incorporated into existing criminal justice agencies or will continue to operate primarily outside the criminal justice system—will have a tremendous impact on offenders. Until these questions are answered, it is hard to say whether the restorative justice movement will be successful in the United States. It is also difficult to predict the effects that restorative justice processes, implemented randomly across fifty states, will have on crime, offenders, communities and victims. The following discussion highlights some of the advantages and disadvantages that may accrue to defendants and offenders as a result of increased reliance on restorative justice processes.

Taking Responsibility Versus Legal Guilt

Before any restorative justice process can begin, offenders must take responsibility for their offenses and admit guilt. In an adversarial process, determining guilt is the chief goal. A virtual minefield of obstacles exists to help the defendant avoid admitting guilt or being convicted, as the State must show in a criminal proceeding that the defendant is indeed guilty beyond a reasonable doubt. The adversarial system allows defendants to believe that they may not have to admit guilt, even if they are guilty, because procedural due process protections will prevent prosecutors and police from forcing them to incriminate themselves. Furthermore, defense attorneys are supposed to ensure that defendants' individual rights are not violated from arrest to trial. They are advised to remain silent, that anything they say will be used against them in a court of law, that any sign of remorse then is a sign of guilt. Their attorneys reinforce the Miranda warnings, advising their clients to remain silent, to refuse to take the stand if their testimony might incriminate them. If a harmful error occurs at trial, such as illegally admitted evidence—that aids a in conviction—the defendant may appeal and have the conviction overturned.

Clearly, the adversarial system encourages defendants to refrain from admitting guilt and instead to have their day in court or to cut a plea bargain that benefits them. Whether found guilty at trial or admitting guilt through a plea bargain, the label of "legal guilt" will follow offenders wherever they go. The stigma that accompanies legal guilt is the rationale for not admitting guilt and not taking responsibility for the harm inflicted on society and victims.

Gerry Johnstone (2002, 89) examines the arguments made by opponents and proponents of the adversarial system. Critics of the adversarial system argue that defendants or offenders become obsessed with exploiting the legal safeguards that mitigate their blame and responsibility. Instead of examining their part in harming another person, they too become victims—seeing themselves as potential victims of an often-unjust legal system. As offenders (as opposed to wrongly accused defendants) struggle to avoid the finding of legal guilt, they disassociate themselves from the crime they committed. Advocates of restorative justice claim that failure to acknowledge moral guilt and to take responsibility for the harm inflicted on others leads to emotionally damaged individuals. Thus, they propose that a system less focused on affixing blame and less harsh on those who take responsibility for their harmful actions should come to the fore.

In his book, *Political Thinking: The Perennial Questions* (1995, 191–198), Glenn Tinder questions whether avenging crime is a proper aim of government. Distinguishing between avenge and revenge, Tinder argues that the destructive passions associated with revenge versus the need for society to right wrongs (avenge) should be considered in the crime control debate. He notes that criminals are to some degree victims—victims of broken families, unemployment, unsafe neighborhoods and so on. Furthermore, he asserts that society must approach the restoration of order and of moral law with the question in mind of whether retributive justice, such as long prison sentences, produces conflict with the former goals and results in the moral destruction of the offender.

According to Gerry Johnstone (2003, 90), the individualistic "legal" guilt sought under an adversarial system conflicts with the offender's view of culpability. The system that forces offenders into court and to admit guilt fails to consider how offenders perceive themselves. Many see themselves as influenced by forces beyond their control, not as free moral agents. Many offenders believe that their fates were sealed early in life, often by circumstances such as abusive home environments, economically unstable households and neighborhoods, and a sense of powerlessness and hopelessness that overwhelmed them. Offenders, then, may not necessarily see themselves as having freely made a socially unacceptable choice. Adversarial, retributive justice may back offenders into a corner, forcing them to put up whatever defense mechanisms they have to shield themselves from harsh judgments and thus to avoid taking responsibility for their offenses.

If being a human being means being connected to and accountable to moral law and taking responsibility for one's actions, then an individual is treated as less than a human being if allowed exemption from the moral order. Hegel (1952, 71) argued that a person is treated disrespectfully if he or she is allowed to break the law without being punished. Under the adversarial system, the central concern is that innocent individuals should never be convicted. And, if that means that the guilty may sometimes go free,—so be it. Restorative justice advocates claim that it's more important for society and for the dignity of human beings that offenders take responsibility for their actions so as to avoid becoming more like animals and emotionally damaged. Offenders would be more likely to take responsibility and admit guilt if the sentencing process or means of reconciliation were less harsh and less retributive in nature.

Widening the Net of Social Control

Numerous scholars have noted the possible net-widening potential of instituting restorative justice processes and programs. By net-widening, they refer to the potential for the criminal justice system to bring in more offenders under community and judicial control than the current system does. In other words, more offenders may be diverted to restorative justice programs as prosecutors and police seek to reduce case loads and specifically among those cases in which strong evidence does not exist to support proof beyond a reasonable doubt.

Systematic evidence of this does not exist in the United States although some modest support for this argument is found in various restorative justice programs in New Zealand, Australia, and Great Britain (Minor and Morrison 1996; Yeats 1997). Net-widening is more likely to occur when police do not take restorative justice programs seriously as a primary part of the justice system and refer cases which they would not address under normal circumstances. Braithwaite (2002, 149) contends that restorative justice does not widen the nets of State social control as much as the net-widening that occurs at the community level. He further argues that net-widening at the community level is not a bad thing. Additionally, Roach (2000, 261) claims that restorative justice programs may actually shrink the nets of State control by diverting cases that otherwise might have resulted in imprisonment.

Reintegrating and Restoring Offenders

In the seminal work, *Crime, Shame and Reintegration* (1999, 26–27), John Braithwaite summarizes evidence on offender restoration through use of restorative justice practices. He finds that most offenders, in case studies examined across the United States, are satisfied with restorative justice conferencing. In 1992, for example, 89 percent of offenders in a cross-site study in the United States reported that the victim-mediation programs they participated in were fair. This compares to the 78 percent who perceived their unmediated cases were handled fairly. Offender satisfaction with victim-offender reconciliation programs in Indiana and Ohio was also high with 83 percent of offenders reporting satisfaction with their experiences. Case studies done in communities outside the United States find similar results. Preliminary evidence suggests that these programs were successful in restoring offenders to the degree that they discouraged further criminal conduct.

At the Weld County Sheriff's Office in Greeley, Colorado, inmates are given the opportunity to participate in an Impact of Crime program. In a classroom setting, former victims discuss their experiences and the consequences of crime in their lives. Offenders then are exposed to the sadness associated with sexual and physical abuse, gang violence, domestic violence, substance abuse, drunken driving, and so on. Confronted with the consequences of their actions, they may weigh the consequences of victimizing others in the future. Implemented in 1999, this program targets offenders whose average length of stay in jail is ten to fifteen days. They participate in a five-day, twenty-hour course and the goal is for them to develop empathy for victims. Facilitators are trained personnel who seek to reinforce social behaviors. Approximately one hundred inmates have completed the program and although recidivism rates are not yet available for these inmates, tracking of inmates reveals that the majority are on probation and parole or have returned successfully to the community (McMahon 2003, 86).

Another measure of reintegration—whether re-entry into the community allows an ex-offender to return to a community as a productive person—requires that the offender-community relationship be characterized by mutual respect, mutual commitment, and intolerance of further deviant behavior. Braithwaite (1989) argues that the community's response to offenders is most important, especially in its use of reintegrative shaming. He notes that cultures that have low crime rates have made successful use of reintegrative shaming which stigmatizes the deviant acts of an offender but not the offender as a human being. Whereas punishment erects barriers between the offender and society, reintegrative shaming allows the community a chance to express disapproval or disappointment that the offender acted out of character, and at the same time, express approval when the offender's true character is restored. Communities in the United States have not been very effective at using shaming in a reintegrative manner. Most shaming penalties in the United States are levied in courtrooms and generally further stigmatize offenders rather than help them reintegrate.

Reduction in Offender Recidivism

One of the measures of success of both the traditional criminal justice system and restorative justice programs is the degree to which they contribute to a reduction in re-offending by the same individual. Braithwaite (2002, 55–56) summarizes a number of studies that link lower recidivism rates to use of restorative justice practices. Among cases involving victim-offender mediation (VOM) in a 1994 study, results show that recidivism is slightly lower in jurisdictions that used VOM than in jurisdictions that did not—although the findings are not statistically significant. In 2000, a follow-up study revealed that of 1,298 cases, recidivism rates for those cases that had undergone mediation were one-third lower than for those offenders who were adjudicated in court. In an experimental evaluation of six restitution programs in the United States, a significant reduction in recidivism was found. In another 2000 experiment, young first-time offenders were assigned to a police conferencing program. Re-arrest among those in the experimental group was 40 percent lower than for those in the control group.

For first-time, nonviolent juvenile offenders, re-arrest is much less likely if they participated in a restorative justice conference. The Hudson Institute examined the cases of 458 juvenile offenders in which 232 had attended restorative justice conferences. The other 226 juveniles were the control group and participated in traditional juvenile justice programs. The study, conducted from September 1, 1997 until September 30, 1999, found that juveniles who participated in restorative justice conferences were 40 percent less likely to re-offend or be re-arrested after six months following their first offense. More than 90 percent of juvenile offenders—who participated in restorative justice conferencing—were satisfied with the way their cases were handled while only 68 percent in the control group were satisfied with the way their cases were handled in the traditional juvenile justice system (Warden 2000, 21).

The results of these and other researchers shows that recidivism is lower among juveniles who participate in victim-offender mediation, and that those who re-offend commit less serious offenses than juveniles who did not participate in victim offender mediation. With juvenile restitution and community service programs, juveniles who participate have lower recidivism rates than those who opted for the traditional justice system (Schiff 1999).

Central City Neighborhoods Partnership, a community conferencing program in Minneapolis consists of a coalition of neighborhood groups, and has been used with 76 offenders over a period of two years as of February 2000. Most of the offenses were nuisance crimes such as panhandling, vandalisms, graffiti, theft, and soliciting prostitutes. A study of the offenders who participated in the community conferencing found that 86 percent of them completed plans to make amends for their offenses and none of those committed new crimes during the two-year period under review in the study. According to the program evaluation, 95 percent of community participants see the program as working effectively and view it as empowering (Walsh 2000, 1B).

One program under scrutiny, the Allen County ReEntry Court Program in Indiana, seeks to help ex-offenders re-enter their communities successfully and thus reduce the recidivism rate. Like much of the nation, approximately 63 percent of Allen County's offenders returned to prison on technical violations or new charges within the first year of their release. In the second year, 78 percent returned and in the third year, 90 percent returned. In a two year pilot program in the southeastern quadrant of Fort Wayne, Indiana, the reentry program was established to address these painful statistics. As of 2002, 80 offenders, exempting those convicted of murder or attempted murder, completed the program. Initial findings show that only 20 percent are re-offending, as opposed to 63 percent of those who did not complete the program (Brockett 2002, 7).

Most of the restorative justice programs in the United States have not been systematically evaluated. Consequently, claims that attribute reductions in offender recidivism to restorative justice must be tentative and modest.

Defendants and Legal Rights

Tony Marshall (1998, 24), in a discussion of restorative justice, argues that constitutional protections of defendants' legal rights are important to protect defendants against false accusation, wrongful conviction, and disproportionate punishment. Without these protections, innocent defendants could plead guilty and agree to diversion to a restorative justice process to avoid prosecution in the traditional system and the threat of a harsher sentence. Consequently, legal safeguards should be in place to assure that defendants are not deprived of legal advice. Marshall further claims that although use of restorative justice practices does not automatically result in a loss of constitutional protections, less attention to full procedural due process could occur.

One of the hallmarks of the adversary system is the idea of zealous representation. Community courts, or problem-solving courts, do not operate on the adversarial "fight theory" premise which holds that two legal adversaries—the defense attorney and the prosecutor—present the merits of the defendant's and the State's case and the judge, as umpire, ensures protection of the defendant's legal rights, a fair trial, and procedural due process. The actors in community courts are not focused on legal rights or on defeating an adversary. Instead the defenders, the prosecutors, and the judges work together to find a plan that will focus on the rehabilitative needs of the offender.

Good problem-solving courts, run by conscientious judges, ensure that offenders are encouraged to seek treatment but not in an overly coercive manner. The cooperation of defense attorneys with community courts is vital because these courts rely on defenders to recommend that their clients participate in their processes. Many defenders argue that offenders benefit if a non-jail disposition or plan for making amends can be devised. Defense attorneys can ensure the rights of defendants who participate in community court processes by levying privacy and confidentiality protections, providing for self-incrimination protections of statements defendants make during treatment, making sure offenders who participate are fully informed about the consequences and procedures used, giving counsel sufficient time to investigate cases before advising clients to participate, maintaining the trial rights of defendants who might be advised to withdraw from participating, and advocating for resource parity with the prosecution ("National Symposium on Indigent Defense 2000: Redefining Leadership for Equal Justice" 2000, 43–45).

Restorative justice principles do not exclude the possibility that defendants may seek legal advice. In many instances, defendants consult with counsel prior to admitting guilt. In the United States, lawyers are present at Real Justice conferences to ensure that the legal rights of juvenile defendants are protected. Defense attorneys can ensure that defendant rights are protected by offering advice and putting procedures in place to ensure that defendants are fully cognizant of the consequences of participating in restorative justice processes (Morris 2002, 601).

Although restorative justice removes lawyers as the primary actors in the justice process, infringement on the rights of defendants is not a foregone conclusion. Other actors, such as judges, are involved in the process and are cognizant of the need to afford legal protections to the accused. Attorneys, at critical points, can advise clients to withdraw from participation in restorative justice alternatives if they feel their clients' rights are compromised. Fully informed defendants can decide whether a restorative justice alternative is best for them.

Protecting offender rights is not the primary objective of restorative justice. Rather, restorative justice advocates believe offenders benefit from participating in restorative justice processes which encourage them to heal, make amends, and reintegrate into society (Morris 2002, 602).

Proportionality in Punishment

In addition to fears about depriving defendants of their rights through a restorative justice process, concerns exist regarding the severity and voluntary nature of community-imposed or victim-imposed sanctions on offenders who participate in restorative justice programs. If restorative justice becomes more widespread in the United States, will the punishments imposed on offenders be proportionate to the offenses committed? In restitution and reparative orders, will emotion rather than seriousness of the offense guide sanctions? If restorative justice programs are the only option, such as Vermont's Community Reparative Boards for nonviolent offenders, proportionality and consistency in sentencing become real issues. Unequal treatment can create injustices and became one of the rationales for backing away from the rehabilitation model.

Ray Schmitz, the County Attorney in Olmstead County, Minnesota voiced doubts that restorative justice programs, such as community conferencing, can be used extensively except for minor offenses. He expressed concern that use of restorative justice could lead to the development of a separate and unequal system of justice for those who admit guilt and turn themselves over to a restorative justice process. Like Schmitz, many civil libertarians fear that two people who commit the same crime under virtually the same circumstances could receive completely different treatment—one receiving full due process and the opportunity to have his or her day in court, perhaps even avoiding punishment; the other is sidelined into a neighborhood justice program composed of overly zealous, payback-oriented citizenry where the offender is ridiculed by the entire community and possibly receives a punishment disproportionate to the offense (Walsh 2000, 1B). Volunteers who work in restorative justice programs argue that "payback" is inconsistent with the ideas of restorative justice and that this runs counter to what actually occurs in community conferencing.

Some advocates of restorative justice programs argue that proportionality is not as important as returning the victim, the offender, and the community to their previous equilibrium. Victim restoration, for example, can occur through symbolic or material restitution. One way to address the proportionality problem is to set upper and lower limits on the plans to make amends or restoration and to limit the amount for which offenders are liable. Other proponents of restorative justice claim that proportionality is not consistent with restorative justice principles. They claim that restorative justice must be judged on other principles and core values such as the degree to which mutual respect is engendered and the feeling of empowerment experienced by victims and communities. Thus, the amount of restitution or requirements for making amends should not be the only issue (Hoyle and Young 2002, 545).

Restorative Justice and Dangerous Defendants

One of the objections to restorative justice is that it will not work with dangerous offenders. Some view this as a serious indictment of restorative justice practices because they argue that it limits the uses of restorative justice programs. Proponents of restorative justice agree that offenders who pose significant risk to society should be imprisoned. They also assert that restorative justice programs can work with dangerous offenders. The use of restorative justice is premised on careful screening of offenders, particularly of those in prison. Preparation of all potential participants is crucial and advocates of restorative justice do not support offender-victim interactions that place the victim in harm's way, psychologically or physically. In the existing programs, seriousness of the offense is one of the factors that is weighed when screening offenders. Another important screening factor is the offender's willingness to accept responsibility for the harm inflicted, the offender's reasons for participating in the program, and the psychological health of the offender (Van Ness and Strong 2002, 186).

In a Salt Lake City justice program called Passages, offenders who participate must admit guilt, receive counseling for six months from a community review panel, and attend mediation with their victims. To qualify for Passages, defendants must have no more than two strikes—or two offenses—on their records and sentences are suspended in lieu of successful completion of the program. After receiving counseling, the offenders meet with victims under the supervision of a certified arbitrator. Upon completion of this stage, the offenders return to community panel supervision which may require them to follow up with social service programs such as substance abuse treatment or anger management classes. A national study found that victim-offender mediation resulted in a 32 percent reduction in recidivism (Khashan 2000, B1).

More frequently, victims of sexual assault, attempted homicide, and survivors of murder victims seek to meet with offenders to communicate the effects of the offense on their lives, to obtain answers to questions that they have, and to attempt to gain perspective on what happened to them and why. Yet, in the mid-1980s in the United States, only a few were provided the chance to engage in VOM. By the end of the twentieth century, victim services units in six states had developed or were developing ways for victim/survivor-offender encounters to occur. The earliest known use of VOM dialogue in severely violent offenses is found in the 1980s with the Genessee County Sheriff's Department in Batavia, New York. Dennis Whitman, director of the program, used VOM to help victims/survivors meet with their offenders. Another early use of mediation between victims of severe violent crimes and incarcerated juvenile offenders is found in Anchorage, Alaska (Umbreit et al. 2003, 125; 127).

Also referred to as Victim-Sensitive Offender Dialogue (VSOD), different approaches have been developed. For example, the Texas VSOD program puts more emphasis on healing and a therapeutic experience. The program in the state of Ohio stresses empowerment of victims and offenders, allowing both offender and victim to define their needs and assume responsibility for meeting those needs. The approach used in Minnesota and Pennsylvania focuses on narrative, allowing each to tell their side of the story and to share the impact of the event on their lives. These programs are usually victim-initiated and victim-driven. Offenders are not coerced to participate. Many of these programs are small but expanding (Umbreit et al. 2003, 128–130).

Of 20 mediated cases in Texas, 70 percent involved homicide; of 21 cases in Ohio, 51 percent were homicides. Of victims interviewed at both sites, 90 percent were very satisfied and ten percent were somewhat satisfied with the experience. Of the offenders interviewed at both sites, 93 percent were very satisfied and seven percent were somewhat satisfied with the meeting (Umbreit et al. 2003, 137–138). These results indicate that, when properly screened, dangerous offenders can not only participate in restorative justice programs, they can do so successfully and with high rates of satisfaction expressed by victims/survivors and offenders.

Conclusions

Defendants who participate in restorative justice programs exhibit high degrees of satisfaction with how their cases were handled and with the experiences they had. Not all defendants, or offenders, are allowed to participate in restorative justice processes due to offender screening and criteria used to determine suitability. Many of the concerns directed at restorative justice processes and the effects they have on defendant rights, proportionality in punishment and the issue of net-widening may be addressed by establishing procedures, limits, and distinct purposes for the usage of restorative justice practices. Some of the payoffs, such as the promise of reduced recidivism and the prospect of successful reintegration of offenders, may attract the attention of the legal and lay communities and induce them to incorporate restorative justice practices in the local administration of justice.

References

Braithwaite, John. 1999. *Crime, Shame and Reintegration*. New York: Cambridge University Press.

Braithwaite, John. 2002. *Restorative Justice and Responsive Regulation*. Oxford: Oxford University Press.

Brockett, Elizabeth. 2002. "ReEntry Court Aims to Reduce Recidvism and Help Ex-Offenders Transition Into the Community." *The Indiana Lawyer* (November 6), p. 7.

Hegel, Georg Wilhelm Friedrich. 1952. *Philosophy of Rights,* trans. T. M. Knox. Oxford: Clarendon Press.

Hoyle, Carolyn, and Richard Young. 2002. "Restorative Justice: Assessing the Prospects and Pitfalls." In *The Handbook of the Criminal Justice Process*. Eds. Mick McConville and Geoffrey Wilson. Oxford: Oxford University Press.

Johnstone, Gerry. 2002. *Restorative Justice: Ideas, Values, Debates*. Portland, OR: Willan Publishing.

Khashan, Nesreen. 2000. "New Justice Program Seeks to Make Whole Victim and Offender; 'Passages' Brings Restorative Justice to Salt Lake City." *Salt Lake City Tribune* (June 5), p. B1.

Kurki, Leena. 2000. "Restorative and Community Justice in the United States." *Crime and Justice* 27: 235–290.

Marshall, Tony F. 1998. "Restorative Justice: An Overview." St. Paul, MN: Center for Restorative Justice & Mediation, Center for Restorative Justice & Peacemaking.

McMahon, Mary E. 2003. "The Impact of Crime Program in Jail Setting." *Corrections Today* 65 (August): 86.

Minor, Kevin I. and J.T. Morrison. 1996. "A Theoretical Study and Critique of Restorative Justice." In *Restorative Justice: International Perspectives*. Eds. Burt Galaway and Joe Hudson. Monsey, NY: Criminal Justice Press.

Morris, Allison. 2002. "Critiquing the Critics: A Brief Response to Critics of Restorative Justice." *British Journal of Criminology* 42: 596–615.

"National Symposium on Indigent Defense 2000: Redefining Leadership for Equal Justice." 2000. Washington, D.C.: Office of Justice Programs.

Neubauer, David W. 2002. *America's Courts and the Criminal Justice System*. Belmont, CA: Wadsworth/Thomson Learning.

Roach, Kent. 2000. "Changing Punishment at the Turn of the Century: Restorative Justice on the Rise." *Canadian Journal of Criminology* 42 (July): 249–80.

Schiff, Mara F. 1999. "The Impact of Restorative Interventions on Juvenile Offenders." In *Restorative Juvenile Justice: Repairing the Harm of Youth Crime*. Eds. Gordon Bazemore and Lode Walgrave. Monsey, NY: Criminal Justice Press.

Umbreit, Mark S., William Bradshaw, and Robert B. Coates. 2003. "Victims of Severe Violence in Dialogue with the Offender: Key Principles, Practices, Outcomes and Implications." In *Restorative Justice in Context: International Practice and Directions*. Eds. Elmar G. M. Weitekamp and Hans-Jurgen Kerner. Portland, OR: Willan Publishing.

Walsh, James. 2000. "Restorative Justice Program in Minneapolis Showing Results; A Study Shows Offenders Who Finished the Program Didn't Reoffend. Some Fear Such Programs Will Create Unequal Justice." *Star Tribune* (February 16), p. 1B.

Warden, Rena. 2000. "Study Shows 40 Percent Drop in Juvenile Repeat Offenses." *The Indiana Lawyer* (September 27), p. 21.

Yeats, Mary Ann. 1997. "'Three Strikes' and Restorative Justice: Dealing with Young Repeat Burglars in Western Australia." *Criminal Law Forum* 8: 369–385.

CHAPTER 3

Restorative Justice and Victims

The earliest criminal prosecutions in the United States were largely private matters. Victims sought either retribution or restitution from the offender and the process was victim-centered. However, the transition from colonies to a federal government led governments to take greater responsibility for criminal prosecutions. After the American Revolution, the philosophy of using criminal prosecutions for deterrence rather than addressing victims' needs emerged. This public criminal prosecution model kept victims at the margins of the criminal justice process until the 1970s. The formation of the victim's movement, which sought greater victim participation in the criminal justice process, sought a shift to the legal priorities of colonial times. This movement led to state and local legislation mandating victims' rights and greater involvement of victims in the justice system (Tobolosky 1999, 21; 26).

Even with the victims' rights movement, victims still feel isolated from the traditional criminal justice proceedings—an emotion compounded by fears of powerlessness and lack of control over case dispositions. In most adversarial hearings, victims, the community, and offenders are not involved in how society will address crime. In fact, with delays and postponements for months and sometimes years, victims may be unaware of the status of their cases. Because between eighty percent and ninety percent of cases are the result of guilty pleas or plea bargains, victims may not be allowed to confront their offenders in jury trials. If trials do occur, more often than not victims find themselves on the defensive as defense attorneys attack their credibility. In this traditional mode of processing criminal justice cases, victims are rarely consulted about their needs or how they believe the case should be resolved (Center for Restorative Justice & Mediation 1996, 9).

Restorative justice, in contrast, involves victims, offenders and communities in a healing process aimed at rehabilitating offenders, restoring victims and making communities whole again. Restorative justice operates on the premise that victims have rights—the right to be heard, the right to participate in the administration of justice, the right to heal, and the right to confront offenders and inform them how their crimes affect them. Restorative justice techniques help victims become involved in the justice process and recover from the trauma of victimization.

Historically, the American justice system concentrated on offenders and only passively recognized victims' concerns. Although offender-directed practices are aimed at protecting society against further victimization, individual victims often felt overlooked and dismissed by a system consumed with large caseloads and paperwork. The victims' rights movement in the 1980s and 1990s has shifted some of the focus onto victims' issues. Restorative justice practices, in conjunction with an increased panoply of victim services, may help empower victims, establish safer communities and create mechanisms to channel victim anger and frustration (Godwin and Seymour 1998).

Victims' rights advocates push for the passage of a Victims Bill of Rights, which outlines a set of protections they believe victims should receive, such as: legal counsel at all stages of the criminal process, information about the prosecution of the case at all stages of the process, reparations for harm incurred and injuries suffered, and the chance to give a victim impact statement once an offender is convicted (Bright 1997). Restorative justice advocates embrace the Victims Bill of Rights as essential to incorporating victims into the justice process. Similar to the Victims Bill of Rights provisions, restorative justice sanctioning practices also include restitution to crime victims, restorative community service, offender payments into a victims service fund, victim impact statements, victim awareness programs, and victim-offender mediation (Bazemore 1999, 89).

Victim Services

Victim services programs play a critical role in helping victims cope with the emotional, psychological, physical, and financial consequences of crime. Victim assistance programs help victims recover from the offense and enable them to go through the criminal justice process. The purposes of victim assistance programs are to provide legal aid to victims of crime, ensure that victims are not neglected, and allow them to successfully reintegrate into society as "whole" individuals.

Victims in the criminal and juvenile service systems may tap into a set of comprehensive services including:

1. an orientation to the criminal justice process
2. presence at criminal justice proceedings
3. the right to be heard in plea negotiations and agreements
4. a Court Advocate who assists victims and witnesses who must testify

5. a victim's aid who calls victims after the first reporting of the crime
6. linkage to social services such as shelters, safe homes, transportation assistance, training and education on victims' issues, and counseling
7. assistance with restitution, compensation, and return of stolen property
8. up-to-date information and notification on case status
9. a liaison who remains in contact with the victim throughout case proceedings
10. encouragement of victim participation in the criminal justice system
11. links to support groups
12. information about community service and other options for addressing the harm of crime (Center for Restorative Justice & Mediation 1996).

These victim services incorporate the restorative justice philosophy by placing more emphasis on the needs of victims and providing linkages to the community as a way of redressing the harm inflicted by crime (Center for Restorative Justice & Mediation 1996).

Victim-Offender Panels

With the rise of the victims' rights movement and Mothers Against Drunk Driving (MADD), victim-offender panels were originally established to help drunk drivers understand the harm caused by their actions on victims and survivors. Victim Offender Panels (VOPs) provide a forum for unrelated victims and offenders, whose only link is the common crime, such as drunk driving, to meet and examine the harms inflicted on the victims and survivors. Both parties share their experiences and the goal is to provide an opportunity for victims and survivors to ask questions of the offenders and to make statements to them. The forum is designed to empower victims and survivors and bring some sense of closure to them. Another rationale behind

VOPs is to reduce repeat offenses by exposing the offenders to the harmful effects of their behavior. Hopefully, offenders will see first-hand the suffering wrought by their actions and will take responsibility for their conduct instead of blaming someone else or attributing the harm to bad luck. Additionally, these panels may force offenders to confront the realities of potential drug or alcohol addiction and break them out of the denial habits they may have developed over the years (Bright 1997).

How Victim-Offender Panels Work

MADD chapters operate VOPs frequently. They rely on judges or probation officers to require drunk driving offenders to attend a panel as a condition of their sentences. Failure to attend brings about sanctions. Three or four victims are chosen to speak about the effects of drunk driving on their lives without blaming or judging the offenders on the panel. A moderator provides order to the panel by supplying guidelines to all panelists and by monitoring the proceeding. Victims do not address the offender who harmed them and do not provide personal information about that particular offender. Dialogue between victims and offenders does not occur unless victims agree to answer offenders' questions. Besides offenders and victims, others may attend the panel such as judges, police officers, probation officers, and individuals who are receiving treatment for alcohol addiction. The other panelists may provide perspectives about how drunk driving affected their lives. MADD-coordinated VOPs require that most of the panelists be victims. Offenders, who are selected to serve on VOPs, must express genuine regret (Bright 1997). MADD's Orange County, California program, started in 1987, has proven therapeutic for the panelists and has allowed families and friends to work through their grief (MADD Orange County—Victim Impact Panels).

St. Joseph County, Indiana established victim impact panels, bringing offenders together with victims, but not their specific victims (Leisure 2002, 10). The Texas Department of

Criminal Justice sponsors victim impact panels that allow victims and survivors to share their victimization experiences with offenders. Victims who have participated express a sense of empowerment and healing (Texas Department of Criminal Justice). In Ada County, Iowa, groups of juveniles meet with victims of juvenile crime to hear the effects of property, business, and battery and assault crimes on victims. These panels attempt to increase juvenile awareness about the ripple effects that their actions have on not just the immediate victim but also on others in the community (Ada County—Victim Impact Program). Victim impact panels are used in driving under the influence (DUI) cases in Lima, Ohio and Putnam County, Ohio to sensitize offenders to the consequences of their actions. Judges indicate that they believe that the panels can make a difference in the future behavior of these DUI offenders (CVS Victim Impact Panels).

Family Group Conferencing

In 1989, conferencing began in New Zealand with the passage of the *Children, Young Persons and Their Families Act*. The origins of conferencing lies with the Maori, aboriginal peoples of New Zealand, who used conferencing to deal with troubled youth. Conferencing involves putting the juvenile in the hands of family, the community, and victims, and allowing these groups to decide what is in the child's best interests and what the appropriate sanction will be. As of 1995, a number of localities in the United States also use conferencing as of 1995. Conferencing is only used when the offender admits guilt. It is not used for purposes of determining guilt and offenders may opt to end conferencing and choose the traditional means of guilt determination or innocence (Bright 1997).

Numerous offenses have been resolved by family group conferencing including drug offenses; vandalism; theft; arson; minor assaults; and, in some instances, child abuse and neglect cases. Like most restorative justice practices, family group conferencing gives victims a chance to discuss the offense and be involved in decisions affecting offender sanctions. It also makes offenders aware of the human toll their crimes have on others and to take responsibility for their actions. Finally, the key support community for both offenders and victims may get involved in ensuring that offenders make amends for their actions and hopefully do not repeat the harmful behavior (Bazemore and Umbreit 2001, 5).

How Family Group Conferencing Works

Conferencing consists of three phases: preparation, the conference, and post-conference monitoring. In the preparation stage, a trained facilitator reads a referral report, talks with other justice officials, and becomes familiar with the case. The mediator meets with the offenders and their family or support group to inquire about the offender's willingness to take responsibility for harms inflicted on victims. Mediators suggest group conferencing as a means of avoiding the judicial process. If offenders agree to participate under the conditions of taking responsibility for their acts and showing remorse, victims and their families or support group are contacted. Victims are told that they have a say in what happens and that courts have not been very good about keeping victims informed about pending court proceedings (Freimann 2001, A3).

At the conference, the victim, the offender, and key members of supportive community groups meet. First, offenders tell their story and victims respond in kind. The facilitator helps them discuss how the crime occurred, how it has affected them, and how the harm can be redressed. During the conference, offenders and victims may ask questions and their respective family members may do the same. The conference process is designed to be tough on the problem, not the person, to condemn the behavior, not the offender. After everyone has spoken the offenders and their families meet to discuss what to do to repair the harm caused by the crimes committed. They put forward an offer to the victim and others in the support community (Center for Restorative Justice and Mediation 1996). Negotiations occur until a consensus is reached and then an agreement is put in writing, specifying the payment and monitoring schedule. In the post-conference phase, the facilitator ensures that the agreement is fulfilled and refers the offender and family to community resources when needed. If the agreement's conditions are not met, the case returns to the traditional court proceeding for resolution (Center for Restorative Justice and Mediation 1996; Bright 1997).

In 1999, Ford County, Illinois implemented family group conferencing. They use it primarily for youthful and first-time adult offenders. In Ford County, the state's attorney forwards potential cases to the probation department. A probation officer then contacts the offender or the parents of a youthful offender to set up an in-home meeting. After talking with the offenders, if they admit guilt, a conference may be arranged if all parties agree to it. At least one community member who was adversely affected by the crime is present. Most conferences last up to one or two hours and each party speaks and may ask questions. Facilitators attempt to reach a restitution agreement that all parties view as fair (Freimann 2001, A3).

Hennepin County, Minnesota under the leadership of Juvenile Judge Robert Blaeser, started family group conferencing in 1999 to place abused or neglected children with relatives instead of shelter and foster care homes. When a child-protection petition is filed, a hearing is held within three days after a child is removed from the home. Family members, who are viewed as desirable candidates, are identified by the county attorney and the public defender. They are asked to help identify which family members could possibly accept the child under their care with the help of a social worker or coordinator. The child may be present and may invite family members to the conference. The family, with the help of a social worker or coordinator, develops a plan which is reviewed, modified, or accepted by the judge (Zack 1999, 1B).

Initial evaluations of family group conferencing are positive Generally, victims and offenders are pleased with conferencing outcomes. However, victims of violent crimes were less pleased than victims of property crime (Kurki 2000, 273). Practitioners observe a reduced fear of crime among victims who participate in conferencing. Conferencing is usually speedier and generates satisfying resolutions in most cases (Bazemore and Umbreit 2001, 6).

Victim-Offender Reconciliation and Mediation

Started as an experiment in Ontario, Canada in the early 1970s, victim-offender mediation (VOM) soon spread to the United States in 1978. An estimated 320 VOM programs exist in the United States while more than 700 have been established in Europe. Victim offender mediation entails a meeting between victim and offender with the assistance of a mediator. Both discuss their perceptions of the offense and the meeting ends with a plan which sets forth steps the offender will take to "make things right" and help the victim overcome the harm suffered from the offense. Usually both participate on a voluntary basis, although offenders may participate solely to avoid a harsher sentence that might otherwise be levied. Mediators do not impose any specific outcome. Their role is to facilitate communication between offenders and victims and to help each achieve a result that both deem fair (Bright 1997). The process is different from mediation in civil matters in that the parties agree about their respective roles in the crime event. Also, the process does not necessarily focus on reaching a settlement, although many do result in a restitution agreement.

How Victim-Offender Mediation Works

Although numerous providers—such as churches, private community based criminal justice agencies, probation offices and dispute resolution centers—exist, standard processes are followed in a typical victim offender mediation event including case referral and intake, preparation for the mediation, conducting the mediation session and a mediation follow-up. Referrals to mediation often come from juvenile court, probation, police departments, and sometimes, local community service organizations or even churches. VOM program administrators do not accept a referral unless the offender admits guilt and shows remorse. Once a referral is made, the case is sent to a mediator (Shenk 2001, 195-196).

The mediator contacts the offender and the victim, meeting individually with them at first to discuss their feelings about the case. This gives the mediator some clues about whether the parties are committed to resolving the dispute and helps the mediator set perimeters about how the session should be conducted.

The mediation session is composed of five parts: 1) the mediator makes an opening statement; 2) the offender and victim tell their respective stories and clarify facts and their feelings about the offense; 3) the victim's losses and options for compensation are reviewed; 4) a written restitution agreement is made; and 5) the mediator makes a closing statement. Once a restitution agreement is drawn up and agreed upon, the meeting ends. Typically a VOM lasts between one to two hours. Finally, follow-up sessions are conducted to monitor and ensure that conditions of the written agreement are fulfilled.

VOM first debuted in the United States in Elkhart, Indiana. Started as an alternative to incarceration, it began a process that brought the offender and the victim together to discuss the effects of the crime on their lives (Leisure 2002, 10). Victim-offender mediation sometimes produces dramatic results. Vicki Crompton, for example, shook the hand of the man who murdered her daughter by stabbing her 66 times after participating in victim-offender mediation. In two sessions, one in 1994 and the other in 1999, Crompton revealed that she and her husband were finally able to ask questions that only the offender—Mike Smith—could answer. For example, the Cromptons wanted to know if their daughter had suffered badly during the attack. Asking these types of questions allowed them to work through their anger and provided a healing experience. (Nevans-Pederson 2001, A3). The Restorative Justice Program of the Frank J. Remington Center at the University of Wisconsin–Madison Law School has transformed Jackie Millar, who was shot in the head and left for dead. Millar, after meeting with one of the young men who tried to kill her, not only has come to care for Joshua Briggs but has also provided testimonials to schools and prisons about the positive aspects of victim- offender mediation (Schneider 2000, 1B).

A relatively new program in McLean County, Illinois has arranged 25 face-to-face victim-offender encounters involving minor crimes. The program's emphasis is on promoting rehabilitation, making the effects of the crime known, and offering the offender a chance for redemption and possible re-entry into the community (Silverman 2002, A1). A program established in Union County, Ohio followed a state law allowing judges to require offenders to meet with their victims to discuss the crime and its effects and to examine the possibilities for restitution or other sanctions for the offense. The program is voluntary for the victim but mandatory for the offender if diverted from court. In Union County, the chief judge decided that offender participation would also be voluntary and that only nonviolent offenders would be allowed to engage in VOM and only after admitting their wrongdoing (Baird 1997, 1A).

A Victim Offender Mediation/Dialogue (VOM/D) program, run by the Texas Department of Corrections, focuses exclusively on extreme violent assault crimes, allowing victims to meet with death row offenders. Like other VOM programs, the offenders must admit guilt and participation by offenders is voluntary. The offenders and victims/ survivors go through extensive preparation with a trained mediator before the one-time, mediated encounter occurs. There is a waiting list of victims/ because of the limited number of volunteers, paid staff, and resources devoted to the program (Colloff 1998, 26). Another similar program was started with violent offenders in Maine State Prison with the primary aim being reconcilation (Harrison 2001, 8).

Satisfaction with VOM is higher for both victims and offenders than those who go through traditional criminal justice proceedings. In addition, restitution was more likely in cases that were handled by VOM. Offenders were also less likely to repeat their offenses if they participated in VOM programs (Arrigo and Schehr 1998). In Salt Lake County, Utah, VOM resulted in a 37.5 percent reduction in recidivism. Nationwide, estimates find that VOM reduces recidivism by 32 percent ("Going Face to Face Brings Reduction in Recidivism Rates" 2000, B1). In a 1990–1991 survey of participants in VOM programs in California, Minnesota, New Mexico, and Texas, 79 percent of victims expressed satisfaction with their VOM meetings (Baird 1997, 1A). Only 57 percent of those who did not undergo mediation were satisfied with their treatment. Over 80 percent perceived the outcome as fair in the mediated programs whereas only 62 percent believed the outcome was fair in the traditional court proceeding. Victims who participated in VOM were also less likely to fear being victimized again (Braithwaite 1999, 23; Bazemore and Umbreit 2001).

Victim Compensation and Restitution

Two approaches were developed in the 1970s to help restore victims and help them heal: victim compensation and restitution. Victim compensation funds are based on the idea that governments should compensate victims for losses incurred by crime. In 1965, the first victim compensation fund was established in the state of California. Other states followed suit and in 1984, Congress passed the Victims of Crime Act which set up a federal crime victim compensation fund. Subsequently, many state legislatures established crime victim funds, providing for the recouping of medical costs and some allowed for recovery of lost earnings of crime victims. Maximum amounts that are paid out to victims range from $10,000 to $25,000 (Parent et al. 1992).

Restitution, starting in the mid-1960s, requires offenders to pay money to victims to restore or make good on something lost or stolen as a result of a crime. Limited primarily to property offenses, it allows for victim input into the sentence and may increase victim satisfaction with the justice system (Davis and Bannister 1995).

Historically, restitution was designed to rehabilitate and benefit offenders, not victims. Viewed as more humane, it also benefitted the criminal justice system by preventing warehousing of offenders and by reintegrating them back into society. In more recent years, restitution has become more victim centered, less concerned with leniency and more oriented toward additional punishment for the offender.

A victim restitution program in Tulsa County, Oklahoma focuses on teaching juvenile offenders the consequences of their actions. Offenders not only make partial or full restitution for the monetary damages arising from their crimes but they also listen to their victims as they elaborate on the effects of the crimes on their lives (Branstetter 2002, A11). The "Earn-it" program in New Hampshire, which began in 1988, requires youthful offenders to pay back the community and the individual or businesses they have harmed. Since the program's inception, 80 percent of the juvenile offenders have not returned to the court system. The administrator of the program screens offenders with their parents and places them in community services sites that correspond to their strengths and interests. The program's success is attributed to its focus on teaching the youthful offenders that crime does not pay but still demonstrating a willingness to reintegrate them into the community (Pugh 1994, 9).

In DuPage County, Illinois, a former police officer, driving under the influence caused an accident that resulted in the severe injury of a 20-year old victim. The former officer was ordered to pay $460,000 in restitution for medical bills resulting from the crash (Rozek 2000, 18). Some jurisdictions, such as the state of Missouri, do not adequately enforce monetary restitution court orders. In 1999, no restitution payments were made in 52 percent of the cases in Missouri (Schlinkmann 2001, D1). In some states, not only may a prisoner's income be used to pay restitution but it may also be used to pay for the costs of incarceration (Hoppin 2000, 4).

Restitution fits well with the goals of restorative justice. It may reduce prison overcrowding (when used in lieu of imprisonment rather than a punishment enhancement). It transfers the burden of victim compensation to the offender. It also may provide beneficial treatment and healing to both victim and offender. Victim restitution in the United States justice systems is difficult because most criminal offenders are poor, making restitution orders hard to enforce. In addition, when offenders are locked up, they are usually unable to honor restitution agreements. Restitution orders and collections are on the rise in some jurisdictions. At the same time, only a few are honored, and those are primarily corporate offenders. Although this option exists on the books, in reality only a small portion of cases are reported and an even smaller proportion of offenders are caught and convicted. This means that in actuality many victims will not benefit from financial restitution (Sarnoff 2001, 34). In 1994, for instance, only 32 percent of violent offenders were ordered to pay restitution. Also, restitution may not meet immediate victims' needs and delay can result in additional victim suffering. Victim compensation programs, paid for by the State, were designed to help victims immediately. Consequently, victims may forego restitution so that they can still receive victim compensation funds from the state. For restitution to mesh well with restorative justice, discussions between the victim and the offender must occur in which they arrive at an agreement on the appropriate restitution order, payment schedule, and how the offender will satisfy the restitution agreement (Sarnoff 2001, 35).

Healing and Sentencing Circles

Healing circles, used by Native Americans and aboriginal peoples in Canada, represent an effort to reintegrate the victim and the offender into the community by providing respect for each individual and caring support systems. Healing circles are private and are formed for either victims or offenders. The victim or offender—for whom healing is sought—decides who will attend. Designed to foster a peacemaking atmosphere, healing circles are typically confidential, and seek to provide an open forum for hearing and understanding the pain experienced by the person undergoing the healing process—which may be either the victim or the offender (Pranis 1997).

Healing circles for victims focus on validating victims—reinforcing supportive principles such as that they did not deserve what happened to them and showing that the community cares about the pain victims experience. Those who participate in victim healing circles help victims express their wishes about how offenders can make amends and assist them in formulating plans for the offender to present at sentencing circles. For offenders, healing circles also involve the community as they discuss the harm caused by the crime and explore paths the offender can take to make amends and to reintegrate into the community as a contributing member. The healing circles of offenders also focus on what should be in the sentencing plan (Pranis 1997).

Sentencing circles consist of all interested parties and seek to bring victims and their supporters, offenders and their supporters, judges, prosecutors, defense attorneys, police, court workers, and all interested community members together to discuss and arrive at a shared understanding of a crime event. The parties then seek ways to address the harm caused by the offense and to prevent future occurrences (Pranis 1997). Sentencing circles came to the United States in 1996 with a pilot project initiated in Minnesota and have since spread in use in a variety of settings, offenses, and offenders (Bazemore and Umbreit 2001, 6).

How Sentencing Circles Work

Sentencing circles involve five steps: 1) the offender applies to participate in the circle, 2) a healing circle is held for the victim, 3) a healing circle is held for the offender, 4) a sentencing circle meets to formulate the sentencing plan, and 5) follow-up circles convene to ensure progress of the offender. Usually, the offenders commit to a plan of action for remedying the ill effects associated with their crimes (Bazemore and Umbreit 200, 6). At the same time, the community, the justice system, offender support groups, and so on also make commitments to help offenders stay on track. Sentencing circles seek to: promote healing of all parties, provide a chance for offenders to make amends, empower everyone by giving each person a voice and by making them part of a constructive solution, address the underlying causes of crime, build communities, foster an ability to work together for positive outcomes and promote community values (Baxemore and Umbreit 2001, 6–7).

The first non-Indian circles in the United States began in Minnesota (Inskip 1999, 11A). The idea has spread to other areas of the country. For example, the Concord Restorative Circle in Massachusetts brings offenders, victims, and the community together to find an appropriate sanction without involving the courts. The program began after circle founders, Jean Bell and Len Wetherbee, became frustrated with the severe measures imposed on first-time offenders in the traditional court setting (Dube 2001, 8). The Community Accountability Circle in Allentown, Pennsylvania allows nonviolent, first-time youthful offenders to atone for and take responsibility for their crimes ("Program Allows Lawbreaking Teens to Avoid Court System" 2001).

Keys to successful implementation of sentencing circles include healthy partnerships between the community and the justice system, trained participants, flexibility, and a high level of community commitment. Ties between the community and the justice system take time to develop. As stronger ties form, grassroots leadership can accept cases, determine how to build support groups for victims and offenders, and supervise the circle processes (Bazemore and Umbreit 2001, 6). Trained participants are essential because consensus-building and peacemaking skills must be learned by all those involved in the sentencing circles. Not all participants are naturally endowed with these skills. Flexibility is required because the sentencing circle process will be molded to some degree by the local culture and resources. Over time, the communities customize sentencing circles to fit their local circumstances. Finally, commitment from community volunteers is essential to the success of sentencing circles. Circles are labor intensive and time consuming, requiring much of citizens. Many argue that circles should not be used to address first-time offenders or minor offenses because of the enormous outlay of community resources (Bazemore and Umbreit 2001, 7).

Victim Impact Statements

An extension of the victims' rights movement, victim impact statements (VIS) represent another avenue for citizen involvement in the administration of justice. Particularly, victim impact statements allow victims to follow through to see that they or their loved ones are vindicated and that offenders receive their due punishment (Long 1995, 194). Victim impact statements consist of victim descriptions of how crime affected their lives or the lives of those they love. These statements give parole and court authorities relevant information on the psychological, physical, and financial effects of crime on victims and those around them. Typically VIS are offered by victims to encourage a maximum or enhanced penalty for defendants (Stevens n.d., 1).

In the United States, every state permits some form of victim impact information at sentencing. Victim impact statements may be given orally in an allocution, in writing, or through audiotape or videotape formats. Most states allow both oral and written statements from victims at sentencing hearings. At the federal level, VIS information is included in the presentence report. In 1994, Congress gave federal victims of violent or sexual assault the right to allocution. At the same time, most states allow defendants to contest remarks made in victim impact statements. Objections are generally limited to perceived factual errors. In a few states, defense attorneys may cross-examine victims about their impact statements. Until 1991, VIS were impermissible in death penalty cases. The 1991 U.S. Supreme Court case of *Payne v. Tennessee* changed this and now victim impact statements are allowed in capital cases. A few states, however, still forbid VIS in death penalty cases ("FYI: Victim Impact Statements" 1999).

As a restorative practice, VIS may hold offenders accountable for crimes or for delinquent acts, promote safer communities by providing information that leads to more responsible case dispositions, and involve victims in a way that is meaningful to them ("Restorative Justice Fact Sheet—Victim Impact Statements"). Defendants, their lawyers, their family, their friends, their ministers, and others are heard in court, recounting childhood abuses or providing reasons why they may have committed their crimes. Victims claim that it is only fair that victims also be heard at sentencing to counterbalance the claims presented by defendants and their proponents (Twist 1999, 377).

Victims' rights organizations often note that victim impact statements are therapeutic and cathartic (Henderson 1999, 406). In a 1996 survey by the National Center for Victims of Crime, eighty percent of 1,300 victims stated that the ability to make victim impact statements at sentencing and at parole was very important to them ("FYI: Victim Impact Statements" 1999). Additionally, VIS may provide critical documentary information about crimes that may be missing from plea agreements, dispositions, sentencing, offender correctional case files. They may also be used to hold offenders accountable for the crimes they committed. They provide a means for victims to present information and to participate in the administration of justice.

How Victim Impact Statements Work

Prosecutors inform victims of their right to provide a VIS to the court. Many jurisdictions give victims a set of forms that describe the type of information most useful to include in the VIS. Since many victims are unfamiliar with criminal justice processes, victim assistance professionals often help victims complete the VIS forms. Typically VIS information is presented orally in court at sentencing. In presentence investigations, probation officials locate victims and put relevant VIS information in their presentence investigations. Later, correctional officials also maintain VIS records as relevant information for parole hearings. Parole boards may take victim impact statements into consideration during their hearings ("Restorative Justice Fact Sheet—Victim Impact Statements").

Critics of VIS argue that victim impact information is difficult to rebut and is overly emotional. Any challenger to a VIS would be perceived as unfeeling and insensitive and opens the defendant up to harsher sentencing imposed by an outraged jury (Stevens n.d., 15). Victim impact statements may lead to revenge-based sentencing, rather than sentences that fit the punishment with the offense. One possible constitutional problem is that when very sympathetic, articulate victims make a VIS, the statement may increase the severity of the punishment. Offenders who commit the same offense may receive widely different sentences due to victim impact statements.

Defense counsels who cross-examine victims may be viewed as hostile to the victim, not simply representing a client. Some analysts argue that the victim impact statement is not cathartic or healing but rather inflicts more pain and trauma on victims who relive the events and are unable to cope with the loss, anger, grief and isolation that they experience (King 2000; Henderson 1999, 14). Some victims may be more articulate than others, causing their defendants to receive harsher penalties for the same offense (Joh

2000). In the capital trial of Timothy McVeigh, the man convicted of the 1995 bombing of the Alfred Murrah federal building in Oklahoma City, victim impact statements were prominent in McVeigh's sentencing and many claimed that the heart-wrenching statements made anything but the death penalty unlikely (Dubber 1999; Robinson 1997, 1B).

Reparative Boards

Used in Vermont since the mid-1990s, reparative boards deal with adult offenders convicted of nonviolent or minor offenses and some have also been used with juvenile offenders (Sinkinson and Broderick 1997). The boards consist of trained citizens who hold public, face-to-face meetings with offenders who are court-ordered to participate in the process. These boards develop sanctions, develop plans and an agreement by which offenders make reparations for their offenses, ensure that the terms of the agreements are honored through subsequent documentation, and issue compliance reports to the courts (Bazemore and Umbreit 2001, 4).

The goals of reparative boards are to: 1) help offenders understand the harmful consequences of their crimes on victims and the community by requiring them to listen to victim accounts or victim reactions to similar crimes describing the harm inflicted on them; 2) find ways to restore the victim and the community; 3) have the offender make amends for the harm caused, and 4) formulate strategies for preventing recidivism among offenders through educational and counseling opportunities (Karp 2001; Bazemore 1999).

How Reparative Boards Work

The reparative boards usually meet in a town hall, public library, or probation office. The setting is much less formal than the typical courtroom. Meetings start with introductions and proceed with a general review of the offense. Boards often hear two cases in one sitting. Citizen members of the boards ask offenders a variety of questions such as: Do you take responsibility for what you have done? How can you pay the community back for what you have done? Are your sorry for what you have done? Board members may also ask questions of victims such as: How did this crime incident affect you? How can the offender make you whole again or make amends? After the questioning, board members go to another room or ask participants to leave so they can deliberate. They return with a probation contract for the offender specifying how offenders will make amends (Karp 2001). If offenders fail to meet the terms of these contracts, they may be charged with violation of probation and referred back to court for more traditional sanctions (Bazemore and Umbreit 2001, 12).

Victim participation in the Vermont reparative boards is now encouraged but was not initially very open to victim input. Some boards seem highly committed to making sure that offenders repay victims. State administrators are also involved in referring victims and offenders to other complementary restorative justice programs such as victim offender mediation and family group conferencing (Bazemore and Umbreit 2001, 4). Karp's observations (2001) of reparative board proceedings indicate that 85 percent of the time they negotiate agreements which require apologies, restitution, and community service. Karp argues that restoration through reparative boards is often "thin"—meaning that criminal harm may be offset by some positive act (such as community service) which is not necessarily linked to repairing the harm caused by the crime itself. Apologies and restitution are generally linked to repairing the harm caused by the crime whereas community service is not directly connected to restoring the victim or making the victim whole. In the absence of victim involvement, the reparative board may lean too much in favor of the offender's perspective and definition of harm becomes unclear. More responsiveness to victim and community needs may improve the success of reparative boards.

Conclusions

Many victims' rights advocates have found a comfortable home in the restorative justice movement. The practices embraced by restorative justice often appeal to the victim's need to be heard, to participate and to be considered by the criminal justice system. Victims experience a sense of empowerment heretofore unprecedented through the restorative justice movement. When the onus is placed on the offender to make amends, to apologize, and to express remorse, victims are bound to remain attracted to this movement and become more involved in the administration of justice.

References

Ada County—Victim Impact Program. < http://www.adaweb.net > (accessed September 27, 2003).

Arrigo, Bruce A., and Robert C. Schehr. 1998. "Restoring Justice for Juveniles: A Critical Analysis of Victim-Offender Mediation." *Justice Quarterly* 15 (4): 629–666.

Baird, Don. 1997. "Crime Victims Get a Chance to Give Offenders an Earful." *Columbus Dispatch* [Ohio] (October 4), p. 1A.

Bazemore, Gordon. 1999. "Will the Juvenile Court System Survive?: The Fork in the Road to Juvenile Court Reform." *Annals of the American Academy of Political and Social Science* 564 (July): 81–106.

Bazemore, Gordon, and Mark Umbreit. 2001. "A Comparison of Four Restorative Conferencing Models." *Juvenile Justice Bulletin.* Washington, D.C.: Office of Justice Programs, Office of Juvenile Justice and Delinquency Prevention (February).

Braithwaite, John. 1999. "Restorative Justice: Assessing Optimistic and Pessimistic Accounts." *Crime & Justice* 25: 1–107.

Branstetter, Ziva. 2002. "Criminals See Victims' Perspective." *Tulsa World* (December 27), p. A11.

Bright, Christopher. 1997. "Conferencing." < www.restorativejustice.org//Rj3/Introduction-Definition/Tutorial/Conferencing.htm > (accessed March 13, 2002).

Center for Restorative Justice & Mediation [Center of Restorative Justice & Peacemaking, 2000]. 1996. *Restorative Justice: For Victims,*

Communities and Offenders. St. Paul, MN: School of Social Work, University of Minnesota.

Colloff, Pamela. 1998. "Contrition: A State-Run Program Lets Criminals Apologize to Their Victims' Families." *Texas Monthly* (August): 26.

CVS Victim Impact Panels. Crime Victim Services, Allen County and Putnam County, Ohio. < http://crimevictimservices.org/ourservices/index/assistance/victimimpactpanels/victimimpactpanels.html > (accessed September 27, 2003).

Davis, Robert, and Tanya Bannister. 1995. "Improving Collection of Court-Ordered Restitution." *Judicature* 79: 30–33.

Dubber, Markus Dirk. 1999. "The Victim in American Penal Law: A Systematic Overview." *Buffalo Criminal Law Review* 3: 3–31.

Dube, Denise. 2001. "Young Offenders Offered Alternative to Court." *Boston Globe* (September 30), p. 8.

Freimann, Michael. 2001. "Ford County Tries New Justice Method." *The Pantagraph* [Bloomington, IL] (January 2), p. A3.

"FYI: Victim Impact Statements," 1999. National Center for Victims of Crime. http://www.ncvc.org/infolink/Info72.htm > (accessed April 2, 2002).

Godwin, Tracy M., and Anne Seymour. 1998. Bringing the Public In: Courts and Communities." In *Community Justice: Concepts and Strategies*. Lexington, KY: American Probation and Parole Association, Council of State Governments, pp. 59–70.

"Going Face to Face Brings a Reduction in Recidivism Rates." 2000. *Deseret News* [Salt Lake City] (January 24), p. B01.

Harrison, Judy. 2001. "Mainer's Peace Found in Prisons; Victim-Offender Work Source of Hope." *Bangor Daily News* [Maine] (May 5), p. 8.

Henderson, Lynne. 1999. "Revisiting Victim's Rights." *Utah Law Review* (1999): 383–442.

Hoppin, Jason. 2000. "9th Circuit: Inmates Can Be Forced to Pay for Prison." *The Legal Intelligencer* (July 14), p. 4.

Inskip, Leonard. 1999. "Restorative Justice, A More Effective Way of Dealing with Crime." *Star Tribune* [Minneapolis] (August 3), p. 11A.

Joh, Elizabeth E. 2000. "Narrating Pain: The Problem with Victim Impact Statements." *Southern California Interdisciplinary Law Journal* 10 (Fall): 17–37.

Karp, David R. 2001. "Harm and Repair: Observing Restorative Justice in Vermont." *Justice Quarterly* 18 (December): 727–757.

King, Rachel. 2000. "Why A Victims' Rights Constitutional Amendment Is a Bad Idea: Practical Experiences from Crime Victims." *University of Cincinnati Law Review* 68 (Winter): 357–402.

Kurki, Leena. 2000. "Restorative and Community Justice in the United States." *Crime & Justice* 27: 235–291.

Leisure, Rena. 2002. "Mediation Can Bring Victim and Offender Together, Allowing Everyone to Move Forward." *The Indiana Lawyer* (July 17), p. 10.

Long, Katie. 1995. "Community Input at Sentencing: Victim's Right or Victim's Revenge?" *Boston University Law Review* 75 (January): 187–229.

MADD Orange County—Victim Impact Panels. Mothers Against Drunk Drivers, Orange County Chapter. < http:www.maddorangecounty.org/vippanels.htm > (accessed September 27, 2003).

Nevans-Pederson, Mary. 2001. "Woman Forgives Man Who Killed Her Daughter, Bitterness Dispelled in a Hug and Many Tears." *Telegraph Herald* [Dubuque, IA] (February 20), p. A3.

Parent, Dale, Barbara Auerbach and Kenneth Carlson. 1992. *Compensating Crime Victims: A Summary of Policies and Practices*. Washington D.C.: National Institute of Justice, U.S. Department of Justice.

Pranis, Kay. 1997. "Peacemaking Circles." *Corrections Today* 59 (December): 72–76.

"Program Allows Lawbreaking Teens to Avoid Court System." 2001. Associated Press State and Local Wire (September 17).

Pugh, David C. 1994. "Work Program Pays Long-Term Dividends; Youth Offenders Earning Respect." *Boston Globe* (April 17), p. 9.

"Restorative Justice Fact Sheet—Victim Impact Statements." n.d. Office of Justice Programs, National Institute of Justice; Office for Victims of Crime; National Institute of Corrections; Office of Juvenile Justice and Delinquency Prevention: U.S. Department of Justice. < http://www.ojp.usdoj.gov/nij.rest-just/CH5/1_impste.htm > (accessed April 2, 2002).

Robinson, Scott. 1997. "Stacking the Deck: Heart Wrenching Victim Impact Statements Make It Virtually Impossible for Jurors to Set Emotion Aside." *Denver Rocky Mountain News* (June 8), p. 1B.

Rozek, Dan. 2000. "Drunken Crash to Cost Former Cop $460,000." *Chicago Sun-Times* (May 3), p. 18.

Sarnoff, Susan. 2001. "Restoring Justice to the Community: A Realistic Goal? *Federal Probation* 65 (June): 33–39.

Schneider, Pat. 2000. "Repairing the Effects of Crime; Programs Bring Together Victims and Offenders." *Capital Times* [Madison, WI] (October 26), p. 1B.

Shenk, Alyssa H. 2001. "Victim-Offender Mediation: The Road to Repairing Hate Crime Injustice." *Ohio State Journal on Dispute Resolution* 17: 185–217.

Silverman, Steve. 2002. "County Weighs Victim-Offender Mediation." *The Pantagraph* [Bloomington, IL] (July 6), p. A1.

Sinkinson, Herbert D., and John J. Broderick. 1997. "Restorative Justice in Vermont—Citizens' Reparative Boards." *Overcrowded Times* 8 (August): 1, 12.

Stevens, Mark. n.d. "Victim Impact Statements Considered in Sentencing: Constitutional Concerns." *California Criminal Law Review* 2: 1–56 (paragraph numbers cited above).

Texas Department of Criminal Justice. Victim Services Division—Victim Impact Panels. <http://www.tdcj.state.tx.us/victim/victim-vctmimpact.htm> (accessed September 27, 2003).

Tobolowsky, Peggy M. 1999. "Victim Participation in the Criminal Justice Process: Fifteen Years After the President's Task Force on Victims of Crime." *New England Journal on Criminal and Civil Confinement* 25 (Winter): 21–105.

Twist, Steven J. 1999. "The Crime Victims' Rights Amendment and Two Good and Perfect Things." *Utah Law Review* (1999): 369–382.

Zack, Margaret. 1999. "Program Will Try to Place Abused Kids with Relatives; It Aims to Cut Time in Shelter or Foster Care." *Star Tribune* [Minneapolis] (July 6), p. 1B.

CHAPTER 4

Restorative Justice and the Courtroom Workgroup

As the courtroom workgroup—police, prosecutors, defense attorneys and judges—use restorative justice techniques, the courtroom culture may change dramatically. The adversarial nature of courtroom proceedings might be reduced as collaborative relationships are formed around the restorative justice model. The concept of community justice, often synonymous with restorative justice, includes community policing, community prosecution, community courts, and problem-solving lawyering. This chapter explores the effects of restorative justice on the courtroom workgroup.

Police

Community Policing/Restorative Policing

Community policing has a variety of meanings. Its major goals include crime prevention and creation of a proactive, problem solving style of policing rather than reactive, control-oriented policing. Other objectives include reducing crime and fear of crime, increasing crime clearance rates and public satisfaction with police services, and building police-community ties that contribute to more efficient and effective policing.

Carl Harbaugh (1998, 116–120) notes that key components of community policing include an emphasis on problem solving, community partnerships, and organizational transformation. In the problem-solving role, police are encouraged to examine the root causes of a problem, rather than just observing its occurrence. He further claims that establishing ties with the community permits police to develop greater sensitivity to community needs and may also help community residents ally themselves with the police. Organizational change means that centralized, hierarchical police departments are supplanted by organizations in which the rank and file officer assumes responsibility for addressing community related concerns.

Community policing requires local solutions to crime, with citizens playing a more prominent role in crime control. Now some police chiefs use community policing to mobilize citizens and to dispel the notion that police own policing. Police organizations, under this model, rely more on informal means of social control. The formation of citizen-police partnerships fosters cooperation between police and citizens on shared concerns (Nicholl 1999, 11). When put into practice, community policing has a dramatic effect on how police operate and how they are perceived by the public.

Various police departments have successfully established partnerships with the community and created viable community watch programs (Dale 2000; Surkiewicz 2000). Still, the evaluation of community policing is not always positive. While crime rates have declined in numerous big cities, civilian complaints about police brutality and misconduct have risen in jurisdictions employing community policing (Willing 1999, 15A). Racial minorities still have negative impressions of police and complain of low response rates (Prine et.al. 2001). Problems exist with carrying the organizational philosophy to the individual level. Often police organizations find it difficult to hire and retain service-oriented professionals who exhibit patience, compassion, empathy, and the ability to communicate effectively—qualities that augur success for most community policing models (Brown 2001). Stereotypes of inner-city residents may also drive some law enforcement officers to fail to use citizens as a valuable resource. To the degree that this occurs, community policing is challenged and undermined. The City Heights Neighborhood Alliance in San Diego, California illustrates a successful community policing venture in which police and community residents have successfully worked together to solve drug-related crimes and to work on quality of life issues in the neighborhood (Stewart-Brown 2001). From most accounts, community policing has much potential and this philosophy pervades many police organizations. Its success depends largely on developing meaningful community ties and transforming police organizational cultures (Weiss and Dresser 1999; Stephens 2001).

Restorative policing builds on the concept of community policing to: promote accountability, reintegrate offenders and heal the community; reduce recidivism and resolve conflict; promote community satisfaction with justice; reduce reliance on formal criminal justice processes; and change police attitudes, role perceptions, and organizational cultures (McCold and Wachtel 1998, 10). It incorporates other approaches to problem solving not necessarily embraced by community policing such as family group conferencing. It utilizes police as facilitators of healing. It too promotes citizen involvement and is being used on an experimental basis in a number of communities.

Citizen Police Academies

Restorative policing ties in with the goals of restorative justice such as citizen empowerment and citizen involvement in problem-solving. For example, citizen police academies may be used to foster greater cooperation between citizens and police. Citizen police academies (CPAs) consist of classes in which participants discuss local police organization and citizens receive hands-on instruction about law enforcement operations. First started in 1985 in Orlando, Florida, CPAs have spread through the United States. Designed to help citizens better understand law enforcement and its mission, CPAs may create greater trust between citizens and police officers and reduce citizen complaints against officers (Aryani 2000). CPAs may give officers a chance to present themselves in a positive light, bridging the gap in understanding that often exists between the citizenry and the police (Maffe, et.al. 1999).

Whether these citizen police academies live up to their potential is a matter of controversy. Critics maintain that CPAs have not lived up to their potential and have not produced equal partnerships between police and citizens. Accused of co-opting citizens for appearances only and engaging in symbolic but surface relationships with citizens, CPAs may only be good public relations (Jordan 2000).

Police-Based Family Group Conferencing

In Bethlehem, Pennsylvania, the police participated in a family group conferencing experiment in which first-time, juvenile offenders convicted of moderately serious offenses were randomly placed in either formal adjudication or family group conferencing. This police-based family group conferencing used specially trained police officers to arrange meetings between the juvenile offenders, their victims, and respective family and friends in an effort to remedy the harm caused by the offender's actions (McCold and Wachtel 1998, 7). Results from the experiment suggest that those who participated in conferences had lower re-arrest rates than those who did not participate.

Prosecutors

Prosecutors, increasing frazzled by jail overcrowding and high caseloads, recognize that their charging decisions, pretrial detention positions, and sentence recommendations often determine the defendant's level of supervision. Frequently, prosecutors operate as gatekeepers of the criminal justice system, controlling case flow and possibly contributing to system breakdown. Various prosecutors have turned to restorative justice practices to reconcile the needs of the victim, the community, and the offender and to remedy harms rather than exact punishment (Gay 2000, 1652). Also, the Justice Department has set aside money for demonstration community prosecution projects in several communities (Jackson 1999, A5).

Pretrial Diversion

Many prosecutors use pretrial diversion as an alternative to formal adjudication. Pretrial diversion has commonalities with restorative justice practice techniques because it: sponsors victim participation, promotes community healing, requires victim restitution, and helps offender rehabilitation, hopefully returning them back to the community as productive citizens. Pretrial diversion assumes that not all criminal violations warrant formal courtroom prosecution. Offenders, however, are not let off the hook. They still have to recognize the consequences of their actions. Pretrial diversion, used for juvenile and adult correctional populations, is different from informal diversion in the following ways: formalized eligibility criteria exist; defendants must participate in a rehabilitative activity such as counseling, educational services, or treatment; and successful participants receive dismissal of all charges. Many diversion programs require community service or restitution (Logan County Diversion 2001; Rice County Attorney: Adult Diversion Program 2001; Pretrial Diversion Program 2001). In Hartford, Connecticut, prosecutors participate in a diversion process in which minor offenders—those who breach the peace, engage in public drinking, or who loiter or litter—are referred to community service rather than prosecuted. A reported 95 percent of all cases are dismissed and the city benefits from the enormous amount of community service generated by these offenders (Kaas 2000, 31–35).

Victim Offender Reconciliation

Prosecutors may refer nonfelony offenders to a Victim Offender Reconciliation Program (VORP). The first victim offender mediation program began in 1978 in Elkhart County, Indiana. By the 1990s, these programs had spread throughout the world, with estimates of 700 in Europe, 200 in the United States, and 26 in Canada (Kurki 2000, 269–270). If defendants exhibit good faith participation in VORP, prosecutors drop or reduce a pending charges and recommend a favorable sentencing option to the court. Offenders in VORP meet with the victims, hear victim impact statements, apologize, and make a restitution plan. In Polk County Attorney's Office, criminal defendants routinely participate in VORP and agreements have been reached in ninety percent of 5,000 cases from 1991 until 2000 (Gay 2000, 1653).

Prosecutors who utilize VORP can reduce their courtroom caseloads. Most victims and offenders report satisfaction with the process. The adversarial proceedings, which often prevent victim-defendant contact, prevent victims from asking questions that only defendants can answer and prevent offenders from exhibiting remorse for their conduct.

Community Prosecution

In the late 1980s and early 1990s, district attorneys and county prosecutors started the community prosecution movement, modeled on the perceived success of community policing. The jurisdictions experimenting with community prosecution range from large metropolitan areas, to mid-size cities, to smaller rural counties. Some employ special units or focus on specific crime categories while others are more decentralized (Gramckow and Mims 1998, 151).

Traditionally, prosecutors operate passively—awaiting cases that police bring to them. Increasingly frustrated with the revolving door and seeing repeat offenders come in and out of the system, prosecutors look to community prosecution as a means of making alliances with community residents to combat crime (Glazer 2000, 1011-1012). The tough on crime image associated with prosecutors also gives them an opportunity to employ softer approaches to crime control. At least 85 district attorneys' offices assign a full time lawyer to neighborhoods and sponsor some type of community prosecution. One in four of 247 police agencies surveyed by the Police Executive Research Forum claimed that prosecutors helped police solve community problems (Glazer 2000, 1026; Park 2001).

According to Coles and Kelling (1999), community prosecution redefines the prosecutor's traditional mission by placing an emphasis on: crime prevention; problem-oriented prosecution; and working more closely with other criminal justice agencies, the private sector, and citizens to reduce crime. With these general goals in place, community prosecution embraces a number of strategies. As an example, Coles and Kelling (1999) use the Safe Neighborhood Initiative (SNI). First created in Boston in 1993, these SNIs create ties between local criminal justice agencies, the local community residents, and prosecutors. SNI prosecutors screen and prosecute cases in neighborhood district courts and targets those offenses which most threaten the neighborhood. Crime rates are lower in many SNI areas, than in non-SNI areas.

Modifications of SNIs include Community Justice Task Force groups, neighborhood association meetings, and neighborhood district attorney programs. All of these place prosecutors in close proximity to the community residents, as they work closely with citizens to reduce crime and address public safety concerns in the community. Highly acclaimed programs, such as the Neighborhood District Attorney's program in Multnomah County (Portland, Oregon) and the Community Prosecution Program in Brooklyn,

New York, are credited with facilitating problem-solving and addressing quality of life issues in these communities (Young 1999, 271). The rapid reduction of crime rates in New York City in the 1990s is in part credited to community partnerships (Park 2001). Neighborhood District Attorneys may serve as facilitators of community participation, suggest ways to create a widely shared vision of a social order in the neighborhoods they serve, coordinate with a variety of criminal justice agencies to assure that aggressive prosecution occurs, and increase community involvement by organizing court watches and keeping victims informed about their case status and their rights (Young 1999, 272).

Some district attorneys ride with police to visit community groups and work with them on their investigations. For example, the Local Intensive Narcotics Enforcement (LINE) Program in Philadelphia represents an intense prosecutorial effort to collaborate with police and combat the drug abuse and drug-dealing problems (Weinstein 1998). Another strategy adopted by proponents of community prosecution involves holding roundtables in junior high and high schools to educate the youth about the effects of vandalism and violence. This grassroots approach is designed to nip the crime problem in the bud, much like the D.A.R.E. programs used by police officers to combat drug abuse (Park 2001).

According to Gramckow and Mims (1998, 159), the work of prosecutors is dramatically changed by becoming involved in community prosecution. When a community prosecution unit solves a community problem and gains trust, the number of lower level crime reports rises. This increases law enforcement effort to clean up a community and improve its quality of life. If prosecutors turn to community prosecution, it may also increase the need to find alternate ways to handle the lower-level disputes such as diversion, treatment, and intermediate sanctions such as probation, community service, and electronic monitoring.

Some prosecutors view community prosecution as too "touchy-feely" and too closely associated with the job of social workers. Still, prosecutors, who are involved in community prosecution, report a rise in community involvement and a surge in crime tips and increased eyewitness participation (Weinstein 1998). Whether the crime rate actually goes down may not matter if residents feel the criminal justice system is more responsive to their needs. Even though the crime rate stays the same, residents may believe that more attention is being paid to their community and that some efforts are being made on their behalf.

Critics of community prosecution fear that it may further erode checks on prosecutorial power and thus lead to abuses of power. They fear that prosecutorial partnerships with police pose threats to ordinary constitutional protections afforded by criminal proceedings. Critics also worry that diversion programs could result in a widening of the net of social control, placing greater numbers of offenders within the reach of prosecutors (Coles and Kelling 1999). The effect of community prosecution on crime rates is unclear. In some jurisdictions, the crime rate actually increased after community prosecution was established; in other jurisdictions, the crime rate has gone down. These decreases in crime rate could be from other reasons; prosecutors could be reaping the benefits of a general nationwide decline in crime (Glazer 2000, 1012–1013). Observations from prosecutors indicate that the concept of community prosecution works to reduce crime and that residents in targeted neighborhoods are grateful for these efforts (Weinstein 1998).

Defense Attorneys

Defense attorneys, typically driven by an adversarial, individualistic model of justice, can expand their conception of justice to a community-oriented model. Public defenders, in particular, already engage in community defense lawyering. The Department of Justice has encouraged problem-solving approaches as part of the defense function, and some private attorneys and public defenders are adopting them. Cait Clarke (2001, 406) offers various illustrations of the problem-solving approach. For instance, a criminal defense team continues to work with a client after the criminal case is over to help him find an apartment, a job, and a drug treatment program. Another illustration is a defense attorney cooperating a social worker, in the best interests of a mentally disturbed client, to locate the appropriate treatment and to address other concerns that will allow the client to reintegrate into the community. When a public defender in California set up a Homeless Court at a homeless shelter where the homeless can resolve their cases and court administrators can reduce case backlog, he showed a way that defense attorneys may engage in constructive creative problem-solving in their communities.

For a defense attorney, the community justice movement means identifying concerns of individual clients or a group of clients and trying to address them by preventing those concerns, be they police brutality or harassment, and working with concerned community members to hold government accountable. Defense attorneys are uniquely qualified to articulate the concerns of clients to government. Those who have set up community justice initiatives rarely consult with public defenders or assigned counsel as equal partners. Defense lawyers who wish to work with law enforcement to problem-solve are frequently not invited to sit down at the table for a discussion (Clarke 2001, 408).

Although the popular image of attorneys is that of trial advocates, this is largely mythical, since most cases do not go to trial. Public defenders spend the bulk of their time and energy in plea bargain negotiations. Many defense attorney leaders seek ways to redress client afflictions such as mental illness, unemployment, and drug or alcohol addiction. Three approaches are possible avenues to explore: 1) whole client representation, 2) defender cooperation with other criminal justice stakeholders, and 3) community outreach activities.

Whole Client Representation

Going beyond advocacy in the courtroom, whole client representation embraces counseling clients in an empathetic manner, helping them develop skills, reaching out to trained social workers to help problem solve, obtaining appropriate sentencing alternatives, and putting the client's current situation in context with the larger community. The defense attorney's use of holistic representation is designed to use the trauma of criminal arrest to change a defendant's way of life (Clarke 2001, 430).

Defense Attorney Collaboration

Defense attorneys can take a leading role in lobbying and influencing criminal justice policy. They may build coalitions and networks to monitor policy implementation. They may communicate to political elites the effects of mandatory sentencing, three-strikes laws, and other policies they deem detrimental to their clients. Public defenders play a critical role in setting up drug court procedures and work with judges to make drug treatment courts functional. They have been instrumental in helping establish mental health courts, community courts, domestic violence courts, and gun courts (Clarke 2001, 442).

Defense Community Outreach

Public defenders increasingly volunteer to teach in local schools and to bolster existing education programs. Some try to reach out by educating others about the effects of race and class on criminal justice administration. For example, the Washington Defender Association works with legislators and public policy experts to improve race relations and rectify socioeconomic disparities in communities. Similarly, the Neighborhood Defender Service of Harlem (NDS) provides legal representation and tries to keep communities in tact by linking individual offenders and their families to the larger community setting (Clarke 2001, 454). They maintain contact with clients after the criminal case ends by linking clients to affordable housing, medical care, and gainful employment. The Bronx Defenders, like the NDS, integrate numerous community members as they represent the indigent community members who are accused of crimes. They create teams of lawyers, social workers, and investigators to represent their clients and seek professional services to assist their clients, families, and the surrounding community (Clarke 2001, 455).

Defense Attorney Ethics and Problem Solving

Some public defenders are heavily criticized for their involvement in community-oriented justice projects. Critics claim that a defense attorney's role as zealous advocate is undermined by the problem-solving approach. They argue that defense attorneys should not sell their clients down the river by committing them to mandated treatment when in court they could vigorously argue and possibly receive a dismissal of the case. They question the ethics of recommending what often turns into longer sentences for their clients when, in fact, through zealous advocacy they could absolve their clients of responsibility for the alleged crimes (Glazer 2000, 1015). Others fear that the collaboration between prosecutor, public defender, and judge—that is required of a problem-solving approach—could result in less zealous advocacy for defendants (Feinblatt and Denckla 2001, 212).

Questions also arise about the role defense attorneys should play in addressing a client's "nonlegal" problems. Defense attorneys are often leery of problem-solving courts because they often define their role as protecting clients from state coercion to the furthest extent (Feinblatt and Denckla 2001, 210). Some fear that the alternative programs and treatment are merely window dressing and will not truly help their clients. Some argue that their responsibility for their client extends beyond the courtroom. They believe that if clients are given an "informed choice" about all their options and if defense counsel has explored all avenues that will keep the client out of prison, the client should be allowed to make an informed decision that is supported by his counsel (Feinblatt and Denckla 2001, 211).

Judges

Triggered in part by guidelines issued by the Commission on Trial Court Performance Standards, judges increasingly are experimenting with the problem-solving approach to their work. Entire state court systems, various trial courts, and numerous individual judges are establishing problem-solving partnerships with other actors in the community. Recognizing that courts may no longer be able to isolate themselves from social problems such as substance abuse, mental illness, and family disintegration, judges are attempting to create more effective ways to handle and dispose of their caseloads (Rottman and Casey 2000).

Unlike traditional judges, judges who adopt restorative justice practices become problem-solvers. Armed with the recognition that both victims and communities suffer losses from crime, they attempt to use punishment as a means of helping defendants by making social services available to them while also paying back the community and giving it a voice in restorative sanctioning. Thus, instead of merely focusing on case processing and punitive sentencing, judges using restorative justice techniques try to formulate sentences that treat the root cause of criminal recidivism and help defendants change their lives (Chase, et al. 2000, 37).

Therapeutic Jurisprudence

More judges are examining the tenets of therapeutic justice. This relatively new legal philosophy holds that judges should utilize insights from mental health and other disciplines to promote therapeutic outcomes in the law. When applying therapeutic jurisprudence, the judge looks at the individual needs of those involved in the case and beyond the specific dispute and case law associated with the dispute. Therapeutic justice focuses on the ability of judges to bring together community resources on behalf of defendants and to link treatment such as drug treatment, medical services, educational assistance, job training, mental health treatment, and other social services to sentencing (Rottman and Casey 2000).

Community Courts

Community courts can involve individual judges, an entire trial court or a state system of trial courts. Ideally, community courts should share the following characteristics: they attempt to restore the community after a crime has been committed; they establish partnerships with the community to make the judicial process visible and accessible; they reach out to community organizations and knit together a fractured criminal justice system; they formulate strategies to help defendants reduce recidivism and community residents deal with the problem of crime; they provide information to all the actors and provide updates on a defendant's progress and compliance with restorative sanctions; and they ensure that the courthouse's physical design reflects the community court's goals and values (Chase, et.al. 2000, 38–39).

Pioneering states involved in court-community collaborations include New York, California, Massachusetts, and New Jersey. Examples of community courts include Midtown Community Court (New York), King County Community Juvenile Court (Seattle), Red Hook Community Justice Center (Brooklyn), and Family Division of the Circuit Court for Baltimore, Maryland. Court planners across the United States are motivated by different concerns and pressures. In Portland, Oregon, for example, the community court emerged as a natural extension of the neighborhood prosecutor program. In West Palm Beach, Florida, the community court started in response to criminal justice system practitioners' frustration with the traditional court model. In Hartford, Connecticut, the desire for greater community involvement in determining what quality-of-life crimes should be prioritized by law enforcement led to the development of a community court (Lee 2000).

The Midtown Community Court in New York City operates with the vision that the Community has a stake in how the courts adjudicate cases and the court's ability to effectively dispose of cases is linked heavily to community involvement. (Rottman 1996). Community groups work with the court to provide outlets for community service and to augment traditional governmental providers of social services. The services generated by community groups such as treatment, health, support, and education are available to residents and offenders alike. A community advisory board and a mediation program were formed to help address disputes within the community (Efkeman and Rottman 1998).

The Red Hook Community Justice Center, located in Brooklyn, is geographically isolated, with seventy percent of its residents living in public housing. The Red Hook court handles low-level felonies and misdemeanors as well as quality-of-life offenses like prostitution or vandalism. Only in operation since June 2000, its successes and failures are not clearly evident yet but many claim that it provides drug treatment and other social services much more quickly than the traditional system (Glazer 2000, 1015).

In King County, Washington, about 5000 juveniles are handled per year by community volunteers in 26 Seattle-area communities. Community committees, made up of between two and four citizens, mete out justice with the victim and juvenile perpetrator present. In addition to community service and counseling, they might require the juvenile offender to write apologies to victims, attend enrichment classes, help with environmental clean-up, steer clear of certain neighborhoods, work at a neighborhood youth center, and other personalized punishment-treatment options. The goal is to teach juvenile offenders that consequences are attached to personal choices (Villa 1996).

The Baltimore City Family Court applies the medical model and practices therapeutic jurisprudence. It upholds the following principles: protecting adults and children from harm, protecting children from the potentially harmful effects of adversarial family law proceedings, increasing access to the courts for unrepresented litigants, promoting early case settlement and referrals to appropriate services, and identifying litigants with signs of substance abuse, and referring them to treatment (Chase et al. 2000, 47–48).

Drug Treatment Courts

Drug treatment courts first emerged in 1989 and since then more than 800 such courts have been started or are in the planning stages. Drug treatment courts share some key characteristics. They involve: integrating treatment and case processing; a nonadversarial means of disposition; identifying and early placement of voluntary participants; providing a variety of treatment services; drug testing; hands-on judicial oversight and monitoring of client treatment; continued interdisciplinary education of judges and other participants; forging partnerships between the courts and other criminal justice, health, and social service agencies; and constant contact and interaction with the community (Goldcamp 2000, 933).

Offenders opting for drug treatment courts forego traditional adjudication and commit themselves to treatment. An incentive for participation may include expunging the drug arrest upon successful completion of the substance abuse treatment plan. In drug treatment courts, the role of the judge is dramatically different from the traditional court setting. Judges must engage with clients directly, ask personal questions, interact with them more frequently, and encourage them throughout the treatment process. Rather than dispassionate umpires who rule on motions and stay neutral in a regular criminal court proceeding, drug court judges are actively involved in the defendant's well-being by contacting relatives, employers, social service providers, and others who may help their client (Nolan 2001, 39–41).

Drug court judges must be community leaders. They must take up the drug court cause and promote it within their communities. They must develop and sustain awareness of the drug court's goals and marshal the resources necessary to support a viable treatment program. Often, drug treatment court judges lobby state and federal legislatures for funding but also seek funding from nonprofit organizations and other nontraditional sources (Nolan 2001, 96–97). Many judges express renewed enthusiasm for their work as a result of becoming drug court judges. Many believe that they are making a difference in the lives of their clients and find their jobs more satisfying as a result (Nolan 2001, 108–109).

Advocates of drug treatment courts also believe that drug courts increase cooperation within communities and among criminal justice related agencies, effectively reduce court backlog, reduce recidivism of drug offenders, and make communities a safer place to live. Some evidence suggests that these beliefs may be true (National Association of Drug Court Professionals and The Office of Community Oriented Policing Services, U.S. Department of Justice 2000).

Critics and Skeptics of Problem-Solving Courts

Some worry that taking a problem-solving approach to resolving legal disputes interferes with the principle of judicial neutrality. The long-standing principle of neutrality holds that judges should be passive umpires and preside over a trial proceeding. Kay and Knipps (1999, 11–12) summarize some of the criticisms of judges who participate in problem-solving courts. Critics of the idea of judges taking problem-solving approaches fear that judges will become social workers rather than neutral adjudicators of disputes. Critics also claim that problem-solving constitutes policymaking and creates an inappropriate role for judges.

Others question whether problem-solving courts will stay on course. Will they return to unfettered judicial discretion and possibly more punitive or coercive approaches as the model adapts and changes? For example if the direction or mood of the country changes to use treatment as a means of levying more punitive sanctions, will these judges and courts also shift their discretion accordingly? Also, will the amount of treatment received be driven by cost-effectiveness concerns? Will concerns about indeterminacy force judges to abandon treatment plans too early (Goldcamp 2000, 951–955)?

It is still too early to determine the answers to these questions, given the lack of opportunity to systematically gather data on how well community courts perform. Some initial results look promising. A 1997 evaluation of Midtown Community Court, relying on focus groups, found that it heightened awareness of and involvement in the administration of justice in low-level crimes; community leaders reacted favorably to it; the general public thought the sentencing practices used there were more constructive; and, from the focus group's perspective, community conditions improved since the court opened (Sviridoff et al. 1997).

Teen Courts

The teen court concept became popular in the 1990s. Usually teen courts are used for juveniles between the ages of ten and sixteen who are first-time offenders and charged with minor crimes (such as shoplifting, disorderly conduct, or vandalism). Teen courts, or youth or peer courts, operate using four different models:

1. The adult judge model employs an adult who serves as judge and rules on courtroom procedure and youth serve as attorneys, jurors, clerks, bailiffs, and so on.
2. The youth judge model is similar to the adult judge model except a youth judge is used.
3. The youth tribunal model allows teen attorneys to present the case to a panel of three youth judges who adjudicate the case for the defendant. No jury is used.
4. The peer jury model does not employ youth attorneys but the case is presented to youth jury by a youth or an adult. The youth jury is allowed to question the defendant directly (Herman 2002).

Teen courts have spread rapidly across the United States. With 78 teen courts operating in 1994, their numbers grew to over 200 by August 2002 and they are present in 46 states and the District of Columbia. The exact date of their emergence has not been established but it is estimated that similar programs have been in operation for at least fifty years (Lucas 2003, 13).

A juvenile may be diverted to teen court only after taking responsibility for the offense and agreeing to teen court diversion. Typically, youth court volunteers process the paperwork associated with each case and schedule the hearings. In programs with youth attorneys, the youthful defendants have a chance to meet with their defense counsel. Youth attorneys explain the hearing procedures, review the facts of the case, examine any mitigating circumstances that might lessen the severity of the punishment and generally prepare the defendant for the courtroom events. In teen court, the youth prosecutor and the youth defense attorney present the facts of the case from the respective viewpoints. In some hearings, victims are allowed to address the court prior to disposition (Butts, Buck and Coggeshall 2002, 5). After hearing from all participants, the judge or judges consider the facts presented to them and review the possible sanctions. In most teen courts, guidelines exist to specify the appropriate range of sanctions for various offenses. After sentencing, the defendant and parents will be told how to comply with the sanctions. Once all components of the court order have been met (such as community service, a written apology, restitution, and so on), the youth defendant will be informed that his or her obligations to teen court have been met (Butts, Buck and Coggeshall 2002, 6).

Estimates hold that teen courts could be handling more than 100,000 cases per year. According to the Office of Juvenile Justice and Delinquency Prevention in 1998, the traditional juvenile justice system processes approximately 750,000 delinquency cases per year. Teen courts have become an important alternative (Butts, Buck and Coggeshall 2002, 2). In a comparison between recidivism rates for juveniles in teen court and similar youth in the traditional juvenile justice system, Butts et al. (2002) found that three out of the four teen courts studied had a lower recidivism rate—about ten percent lower—after six months than that of the comparison group. This four-state study revealed that six to nine percent of teen court defendants re-offended within six months while 18 percent of those processed by the traditional juvenile courts re-offended (Lucas 2003, 13). Other studies have found recidivism rates of twenty or thirty percent. An analysis of Arlington, Texas teen court compared recidivism among teen court defendants with a group of teens matched on sex, race, age, and offense who were non-teen-court participants. This study found that teen court participants were less likely to re-offend, but that they still had a 24 percent recidivism rate while the non-teen-court participants had a 36 percent recidivism rate ("Teen Courts: A Focus on Research" 2002, 4). These preliminary findings indicate that teen courts may be promising alternatives for handling juvenile offenses.

Besides possibly lowering recidivism, teen courts also offer other benefits. Teen courts, by requiring youthful offenders to take responsibility for their illegal actions, ensure accountability. They also process cases much more quickly, moving youth offenders from arrest to sanction in a few days, rather than taking months to respond. If managed properly, they are less costly than the traditional juvenile court system. They may also bring about greater community cohesion and better community-court relationships ("Teen Courts: A Focus on Research" 2000). Teen courts meet restorative justice goals by encouraging community involvement in resolving issues associated with crime, by encouraging youthful offenders to take responsibility for their actions, and by successfully reintegrating many youthful offenders back into the community.

Although teen courts offer advantages, they also face challenges and obstacles to widespread implementation. First, a significant number of teen courts are inhibited by funding uncertainties. Recruiting and retaining youth volunteers is another obstacle. Teen courts report that in some cases too much time passed between a youth's arrest and referral to teen court. They also claim that it is difficult to coordinate teen court efforts with support agencies in the community ("Teen Courts: A Focus on Research" 2000).

Conclusions

Restorative justice techniques change the dynamic of the operations of the courtroom workgroup and alter their behavior in ways that might benefit the community. Closer community ties developed through police, prosecutor, defense attorney, and judge partnerships augur greater satisfaction with, and understanding of, the administration of justice. Also, these ties may lead to more fruitful resolutions to crime and more useful ways to redress the harm inflicted on communities by criminal acts. Often actors in the courtroom workgroup, who utilize restorative justice techniques, speak of empowerment and greater satisfaction with their jobs. As more experimentation occurs in the United States, communities and the courtroom workgroup may transform the justice system in its treatment of low-level offenders.

References

Aryani, Giant Abutalebi, Terry D. Garrett, and Carl L. Alsabrook. 2000. "The Citizen Police Academy: Success Through Community Partnerships." *FBI Law Enforcement Bulletin* 69 (May): 16–21.

Brown, Jim. 2001. "Community Policing Reality Check." *Law & Order* 49 (April): 55–58.

Butts, Jeffrey A., Janeen Buck, and Mark B. Coggeshall. April 2002. "The Impact of Teen Court on Young Offenders." Washington, D.C.: The Urban Institute, Justice Policy Center.

Chase, Deborah J., Hon. Sue Alexander, and Hon. Barbara J. Miller. 2000. "Courts Responding to Communities: Community Courts and Family Law." *Journal of the Center for Children & the Courts* 2: 37–54.

Clarke, Cait. 2001. "Problem-Solving Defenders in the Community: Expanding the Conceptual and Institutional Boundaries of Providing Counsel to the Poor." *Georgetown Journal of Legal Ethics* 14 (Winter): 401–458.

Coles, Catherine M., and George L. Kelling. 1999. "Prevention through Community Prosecution." *Public Interest* 136 (Summer): 69–84.

Dale, Nancy. 2000. "Turning Around an Agency: How the Fort Pierce Police Department Did It." *Law & Order* 48 (November): 87–91.

Efkeman, Hillery S., and David B. Rottman. 1998. Bringing the Public In: Courts and Communities." In *Community Justice: Concepts and Strategies*. Lexington, KY: American Probation and Parole Association, Council of State Governments, pp. 131–149.

Feinblatt, John, and Derek Denckla. 2001. "What Does It Mean to Be a Good Lawyer? Prosecutors, Defenders and Problem-Solving." *Judicature* 84 (January/February): 206–214.

Gay, Frederick W. 2000. "Restorative Justice and the Prosecutor." *Fordham Urban Law Journal* 27 (June): 1651–1662.

Glazer, Sarah. 2000. "Community Prosecution: Should Prosecutors Try to Solve Local Problems?" *CQ Researcher* 10: 42 (December 15, 2000): 1009–1032.

Goldcamp, John S. 2000. "The Drug Court Response: Issues and Implications for Justice Change." *Albany Law Review* 63: 923–961.

Gramckow, Heike P,. and Rhonda Mims. 1998. *Community Justice: Concepts and Strategies*. Lexington, KY: American Probation and Parole Association, Council of State Governments, pp. 151–161.

Harbaugh, Carl R. 1998. "Community Policing: An Evolution Back to the Basics." In *Community Justice: Concepts and Strategies*. Lexington, KY: American Probation and Parole Association, Council of State Governments, pp. 113–129.

Herman, Madelynn M. 2002. "Juvenile Justice Trends in 2002 Teen Courts: A Juvenile Justice Diversion Program." National Center of State Courts, Knowledge and Information Services.

Jackson, Robert L. 1999. "Community Prosecuting Wins Fans, Federal Funds." *Los Angeles Times* (March 30), p. A5.

Jordan, W.T. 2000. "Citizen Police Academies: Community Policing or Community Politics? *American Journal of Criminal Justice* 25 (Fall): 93–105.

Kaas, Glenn M. 2000. "Restorative Justice: A New Paradigm for the Prosecutor (A View from Hartford Community Court)." *Prosecutor* 34 (November–December 2000): 31–35.

Kaye, Judith S., and Susan K. Knipps. 1999/2000. "Judicial Responses to Domestic Violence: The Case for a Problem Solving Approach." *Western State University Law Review* 27: 1–13.

Lee, Eric. 2000. "Community Courts: An Evolving Model." Washington, D.C.: Office of Justice Programs, U.S. Department of Justice.

"Logan County Diversion." 2001. < http://www.co.logan.oh.us/prosecutor/diversion.htm > (accessed Octobern 21, 2001).

Lucas, Kelly. 2003. "Teen Courts Give Kids Second Chance: Youth Diversion Program Encourages Reparation to Avoid Criminal Charges." *The Indiana Lawyer* (June 18), p. 13.

Maffe, Steven R., and Tod W. Burke. 1999. "Citizen Police Academies." *Law & Order* 47 (October): 77–80.

McCold, Paul, and Benjamin Wachtel. 1998. *Restorative Policing Experiment: The Bethlehem Pennsylvania Police Family Group Conferencing Project*. Pipersville, PA: Community Service Foundation.

National Association of Drug Court Professionals and The Office of Community Oriented Policing Services, U.S. Department of Justice. 2000. "Developing Linkages Between Law Enforcement and the Courts: Community Policing and Drug Courts/Community Courts Project." Washington, D.C.: U.S. Department of Justice.

Nolan, James L., Jr. 2001. *Reinventing Justice: The American Drug Court Movement*. Princeton: Princeton University Press.

Park, Paula. 2001. "DAs Still Getting Out on Street: After 10 Years, Community Prosecution Is Growing; Some Worry About Funding." *American Bar Association Journal* 87: 26.

"Pretrial Diversion Program." 2001. < http://www.grantda.org/pretrial diversion.html > (accessed October 21, 2001).

Prine, Rudy K., Chet Ballard, and Deborah M. Robinson. 2001. "Perceptions of Community Policing in a Small Town." *American Journal of Criminal Justice* 25 (Spring): 211–221.

"Rice County Attorney: Adult Diversion Program." 2001. < http://www.co.rice.mn.us/Attorney/AdultDiversion.htm > (accessed October 21, 2001).

Rottman, David B. 1996. "Community Courts" Prospects and Limits." *National Institute of Justice Journal* Issue No. 231 (August): 46–51.

Rottman, David and Pamela Casey. 2000. "Therapeutic Jurisprudence and the Emergence of Problem-Solving Courts." *Corrections Forum* 9 (March/April): 27–30.

Stephens, Gene. 2001. "Proactive Policing: The Key to Successful Crime Prevention and Control." *USA Today* 129 (May): 32.

Stewart-Brown, Recheal. 2001. "Community Mobilization: The Foundation of Community Policing." *FBI Law Enforcement Bulletin* 70 (June): 9–17.

Surkiewicz, Joe. 2000. "Community-Based Policing Isn't Easy, But Proponents Say It's Working in Park Heights." *The Daily Record* [Baltimore] (April 29).

Sviridoff, Michele, David Rottman, Brian Ostrom, and Richard Curtis. 1997. *Dispensing Justice Locally: The Implementation and Effects of the Midtown Community Court*. Washington, D.C.: National Institute of Justice, Office of Justice Programs, U.S. Department of Justice (May).

"Teen Courts: A Focus on Research." 2000. *Juvenile Justice Bulletin* (October) < http://www.ncjrs.org/html/ojjdp/jjbul2000_10_2/ intro.html > (accessed September 22, 2003).

Villa, Judy. "Juvenile Justice: Community Courts." *Arizona Republic* (November 6, 1996).

Weinstein, Susan P. 1998. "Community Prosecution: Community Policing's Legal Partner." *FBI Law Enforcement Bulletin* 67 (April): 19–24.

Weiss, Jim, and Mary Dresser. 1999. "Cop: The Policing Revolution at Work in the Real World." *Police* 23 (August): 26–31.

Willing, Richard. 1999. "Community Policing Passes the 'Fort Apache' Test." *USA Today* (June 15), p. 15A.

Young, Marlene A. 1999. "Restorative Community Justice in the United States: A New Paradigm." *International Review of Victimology* 6: 265–277.

CHAPTER 5

Restorative Justice and the Community

Defining Community

The terms, "community" and "neighborhood," are often used interchangeably. Technically, however, the words have different meanings. A neighborhood refers to a particular geographic area that is part of a larger jurisdiction. Boundaries of the neighborhood are loosely defined as we refer to the west side of Chicago or south-central Los Angeles. Residents may understand these as coherent neighborhoods but may not be able to precisely locate their actual boundaries. Community, on the other hand, may refer to a neighborhood but it often denotes people rather than places.

Even when community is a neighborhood, such as the New Haven community or the Soho community, we think of the people who live and work in these places rather than a simple location (Clear and Cadora 2003, 7). In addition, community may not only signify a place but may also connote a group identity such as the Eurasian community or the African-American community. According to Clear and Cadora (2003, 8), when thought of this way, community refers to a collection of people who see themselves as belonging together even though they may not be located in the same geographic area.

Communities and neighborhoods are viewed similarly in the United States because people who share common identities or backgrounds often live near each other. Many immigrant populations, as demonstrated by Little Italy or Chinatown, find it more comfortable to live among others of similar background and language while others feel they might not be allowed to live among others unlike them. Differences from one community to another suggest that criminal justice strategies should be designed to address and conform to these differences. Community justice advocates argue that more focus on places, not cases, is key. Making communities a better place to live by helping residents reclaim their public space and organizing residents for crime prevention is central to the tenets of community justice (Clear and Cadora 2003, 15).

Determining the "relevant" community may not always be clearcut. In restorative justice, the relevant community does not exist prior to the commission of a crime. After a crime is committed, community is often defined by the level of harm inflicted, the victim-offender relationship and the number of individuals affected by the crime. Often, it may be difficult, if not impossible, to involve all members of a community who were indirectly and directly affected by an offense. This leads many advocates of restorative justice to argue for a more narrow drawing of community boundaries and to include only those directly affected by the crime in the restorative justice process. Practically speaking, questions about who constitutes the relevant community for a specific conflict are best resolved by examining the roles and responsibilities of communities in a restorative criminal justice process (Johnstone 2002).

Pranis (n.d.) contends that community of place is of utmost importance. Although we function in different communities, such as schools, families, churches, and so on, community of place is most salient because crime generally affects those living in a particular geographic space. Those closest to a crime reside in that community of place and are most affected by it even if they bear no immediate relationship to the victim. Thus, those in a geographic community have the most at stake. Furthermore, in urban communities, many residents do not possess the means to pull up stakes and move out. Not having this ability to choose where they will live limits them to community of place—a geographic area in which they live. This makes community of place primary to them. Children, too, are affected greatly by the place in which they are raised. Their experiences in the community of place will have a profound impact on them even with nongeographical influences and communities in their lives. Studies show that community of place is related to delinquent behavior and thus community of place is important to crime prevention efforts. Finally, for most people, their sense of safety and order is linked to a geographic community.

Community Justice and Crime

Community justice and restorative justice are interrelated. They both share the fundamental notion that crime is a social problem, not just an individual aberration, and crime affects the quality of life in all communities. Both community justice and restorative justice hold that focusing on crime, after it has occurred, is the least productive way to manage this social problem. Rather than focusing on what should happen to offenders after they work their way into the traditional justice system, they argue, we should focus on crime prevention, rather than on arresting, prosecuting, adjudicating, and punishing offenders.

Community justice proponents argue for building a sense of community through citizen involvement in which communities cooperate and work with criminal justice agencies to prevent crime. Accordingly, most restorative justice programs center around the community. Restorative justice, however, allows equal involvement for victims, offenders, and communities in decision-making, whereas community justice does not always address the roles of victims and offenders directly (Kurki 2000, 237).

Communities of Interest and Responsibility

Rather than giving the State primacy in the administration of justice, restorative justice advocates wish to return justice and punishment functions to the victims, offenders, and their communities of interest. Morris and Young (2000, 14) define communities of interests as a group of individuals with shared concerns about the offender, victim, and the offense's impact, who also have the ability to engage in problem-solving activities directed at crime. Communities of interest can provide support to victims and offenders as they discuss the appropriate responses to offenses.

The locus of responsibility in restorative justice is communities of interest, which takes away the State's monopoly over justice decision-making. Whereas the traditional justice system gives power to legal experts, such as judges, defense attorneys, and prosecutors, restorative justice encourages collective responsibility in the communities of interest. At its foundation, restorative justice holds that shared values in these communities of interest should be used to address crime and its effects. Furthermore, reintegration of victims and offenders into the community fold should occur at the local community level.

Community Involvement in Restorative Justice

In the traditional justice system employed in the United States, the community is currently represented by the State. In a restorative justice system, the community takes a much more active role. Whereas the State represents the people in the traditional justice system, the people represent their own interests in a restorative justice system. Under restorative justice, a larger number of lay people must be ready and willing to take a proactive role in the administration of justice. Foundational to restorative justice is the assumption that the offender's community has the greatest influence over the offender and may influence him or her to repair the harm inflicted or to restrain from future criminal behavior. At the same time, the community is the support base on which offenders rely as they try to re-enter society as law-abiding citizens. Consequently, to support restorative justice values, the community is essential to making restorative justice a reality (Johnstone 2002, 152).

Nils Christie (1977) argues that community involvement in resolution of conflict and problem-solving is extremely important. His article, "Conflicts as Property," provides some of the underpinnings of restorative justice theory and practice. In this article, Christie makes four arguments that are important to our discussion:

1. The handling of conflict is an important social act. Conflict in industrialized societies has become invisible and incomprehensible (1977, 1).
2. The parties involved in conflicts no longer own them as they have been taken over by the State, primarily legal experts and criminal justice professionals (1977, 1,4)
3. Victims, in particular, have lost in this process as they have been excised from their right to fully participate in conflict resolution proceedings (1977, 3).

4. Conflicts are the property of communities and community-based processes should be in place to address them (1977, 12).

For many advocates of restorative justice, the community is often portrayed as a secondary victim of crime. When a community is adversely affected by crime, it should have the right to address the crime and the issues raised for the community. The community, as stakeholders, should have input into solving the community problem of crime (Crawford 2002, 118). Others claim that community involvement in conflict processing promotes civic responsibility and a politically engaged citizenry. Community involvement becomes a tool for a more deliberative type of justice in which citizens discuss the consequences of crime and how to address it. Ordinary citizens can mitigate bureaucratic responses to crime and humanize the administration of justice (Crawford 2002, 119–120).

Critics of restorative justice contend that the lack of a real sense of community in modern societies makes restorative justice unrealistic. Furthermore, they assert that it is impractical because of the difficulties associated with attracting layperson volunteers (Crawford 2002, 121). In fact, some lay people are co-opted by legal technicians and lose their unique qualities and responsiveness to values in the community. Community involvement can be dangerous to promoting social justice as parochial interests may conflict with larger social goals. Involvement of lay people leads to conflict of interest problems, lack of neutrality, and threats to decision-making legitimacy (Crawford 2002, 122–123).

Involving communities is not as easy as making opportunities available and assuming that community members will come. In modern, urban societies, people must be persuaded that their involvement is important. Because criminal justice is viewed as punishment, many citizens may not want to become involved due to the distaste they associate with inflicting pain on someone or due to fears that they may be recipients of retaliation from those punished. From this viewpoint, it is easier to let correctional professionals deal with the crime problem rather than taking time out of work and leisure to address the issue (Johnstone 2002, 153).

Another problem with community involvement is determining whose community interests are at stake. What counts as community stakeholders can vary greatly. Potentially, the entire nation could be directly involved in a criminal justice case if the restorative justice argument is taken to its extreme logic. For example, a serial killer who crosses state lines and has murdered in numerous states may be an instance in which the whole country has a stake in the case's resolution. Similarly, it is hard to determine where the boundary of community ends in white-collar crimes that afflict thousands of harmed individuals. If the definition of community is limited only to those harmed, it is still difficult to pinpoint community interests and whose interests have been violated (Johnstone 2002, 155).

Despite the problems of defining communities and engaging communities in restorative justice processes, proponents of restorative justice claim that involving lay people in the administration of justice strengthens community ties. In their view, the lack of opportunity for lay participation in the justice process is one of the explanations for why modern communities are weak. Thus, the weaker the community is, the greater the need to involve ordinary citizens in the justice process (Cayley 1998, 168). Consequently, they advocate establishing microcommunities, as well as personal communities of victims and offenders, to promote healing and reintegration (McCold and Wachtel 2002, 46). They further contend that academic definitions of community will never be precise. Practical experience in establishing restorative processes in communities suggests that these definitions do not have to be precise to work with communities. Communities involve not just an individual's responsibilities to others but also the responsibility of others in the community to individuals; communities must respect and honor the needs of individuals and the needs of the group (Pranis n.d.).

Diverting Criminal Cases to Community Groups

One way to make restorative justice more attractive to those who hold political power is to emphasize its cost-saving potential. Roach (2000, 268) argues that one of the reasons why restorative justice has become a more frequent item in public discourse is due to its potential ability to cut the costs of administering justice. In times of budget shortfalls and budget deficits faced by many state governments as they enter the twenty-first century, the ability to save public monies is attractive. Allowing community groups to handle some criminal cases may privatize, at least in part, a key state function.

Those fearful of the current trend toward the privatization of State functions assert that its primary emphasis is on efficiency with less concern for upholding important constitutional protections or precedents that protect individual liberties. Although restorative justice may be amendable to privatization, or to the turning over of traditional government functions to private citizens or organizations, this alone is not sufficient to reject its usage. In some cases, community organizations may be better able to provide services to offenders and victims who may already distrust the state (Roach 2000, 268).

Numerous scholars note that faith-based communities are potential agents for reintegrating—helping both victims and offenders (McHugh 1978; Cnaan et al. 1999; McKelvey 1977). Crisis services for victims can help them address issues such as how to cope with their feelings; how to navigate the criminal justice process; how to get access to food, clothing, shelter, and financial aid; and generally how to heal (Van Ness and Strong 2002, 118). Offenders making a transition back to communities may need transition skills, coping skills, and mentoring. Faith-based organizations have become involved in job training, drug and alcohol treatment, halfway houses, and life skills training. Whereas government programs are limited in their ability to help victims and offenders with spiritual and faith issues, faith-based organizations may provide spiritual and emotional support that help both victim and offender find suitable support networks (Van Ness and Strong 2002, 119–120).

Civil libertarians express particular concern over the use of faith-based private organizations for the delivery of services traditionally provided by government. Currently, charitable faith-based organizations provide an array of social services from mentoring inner city youth to counseling drug addicts. Some fear that charitable choice organizations will result in the advancement of state-supported religion. If a faith-based drug abuse outreach program such as Teen Challenge received state funds, for instance, a constitutional challenge could ensue because this program puts forth the idea that a commitment to Jesus Christ will fill an emptiness in the soul formerly filled by drug use. If government funded this program, it would be promoting a specific religious viewpoint. Various scholars believe this separation of church and state issue may render many faith-based initiatives unconstitutional. Additionally, the performance of faith-based organizations compared to secular ones is not necessarily better (Glazer 2001, 380). The implications for faith-based restorative justice programs are unclear. However, to the extent that offenders are diverted by the State into these programs, church-state issues will probably arise.

Still, community groups and organizations are positioned, in many instances, to deliver services not only efficiently, but also effectively. Because the State often plays a role in funding these programs, it can ensure that important values such as fairness, equal treatment and accessibility are upheld. It also may hold community groups accountable for restorative justice proceedings that do not comply with cherished values and principles (Roach 2000, 269). The degree to which diversion of criminal cases to the community occurs will depend on how willing society is to marginalize the value of punishment and to rely on restorative processes. The level of funding and sustained community support for restorative justice processes as mechanisms for crime prevention will be key (Braithwaite 1999, 1749).

Community Empowerment

Restorative justice theorists argue that the closer the problem solvers (in the case of the traditional justice system, the adjudicators) and enforcers of norms are to offenders, the more effective they are in bringing about a desired change in the behavior of offenders (Ashworth 2002, 582). Some theorists maintain that formal social control mechanisms, such as those embodied in the criminal justice system, are not as effective as informal social controls, such as family, friends, neighbors, and social organizations (Clear and Cadora 2003, 1-2). Restorative justice advocates argue that communities are empowered when they have the capacity to regulate themselves. As Cayley (1998, 168) notes, when justice becomes professionalized and the communities are robbed of their abilities to address conflicts, communities actually lose their ability to restore order and keep the peace.

Getting those closest to offenders and victims involved in justice administration may reduce crime and the fear of crime. Restorative justice advocates contend that through greater social contact, a sense of community is generated giving friends, neighbors, and social organizations more informal social control. This sense of solidarity contributes to a sense of peace and less fear of crime. One example, the Chicago Area Project (CAP), became a model for community action. CAP sought to improve neighborhood conditions in six areas of Chicago by reaching out to delinquents and gang members and setting up recreational programs for children. CAP was most successful in neighborhoods that were more stable and ethnically homogeneous (Hope 1995, 27-29).

Developing social capital or the ability to work with one's neighbor, such as picking up each other's mail while one is away on vacation or plowing a neighbor's road after a big snow without expecting something in return, creates the conditions for informal social control. Informal control may be extended through neighborhood watch associations, community meetings and so on (Sampson 1999). Evidence suggests that fear of crime and disorder can be an issue that mobilizes community action. Whether the action can be sustained is a question of concern. Research indicates that efforts to increase social control, neighborhood cohesion, and volunteerism have not been so successful in the United States (Moore 1999). Sampson (1999, 271) suggests that using community to change individual behaviors is among the hardest things to do.

Proponents of restorative justice believe that community empowerment is possible through greater collaboration between criminal justice agencies and ordinary citizens. If they work closely together, more crime prevention and better crime solving is likely. They stress the importance of making citizens active rather than passive; in other words, they are not just service recipients but actually have real power and are included in problem-solving and decision-making processes that make a difference (Kurki 2000, 245). They further contend that restorative justice processes provide the forum for citizen deliberations about the consequences of crime. Informed public debate and conversations about how to resolve conflicts creates reasoned community participation and may deter a knee-jerk punitive response to crime (Crawford 2002, 118–119).

Critics contend that restorative justice techniques are not always empowering. If a program is poorly implemented, lacks adequately trained facilitators or has an inadequately defined vision, conferences between victims and offenders may fail and offenders go on to re-offend. Various studies show that family group conferences, often hailed as successful by restorative justice advocates, have failed in a high number of cases. In samples studies by Maxwell and Morris in 1993 and 1997, 41 percent of victims did not attend family group conferences either because they were not invited or were not given sufficient notice and of those who attended. Forty-nine percent expressed some satisfaction with the outcome. Only one-third of victims stated that they felt better as a result of conferencing, and 25 percent felt worse as a result. Surveys of young offenders also yielded disappointing results with only one-third saying that they felt involved, with about two-thirds of them re-offending after four years and about a quarter of them re-convicted during this time (Barton 2000, 69–70). These data indicate that restorative justice techniques may fall short of the goal of community empowerment.

Although restorative justice advocates endorse an inclusive approach to defining "community," critics argue that, in practice, the real restorative justice vision of community is very narrow, encompassing only the families of victims and offenders. They further claim that justice administered at the local level results in justice by geography with wide variations in standards, resulting in inconsistency and a possible sacrifice of the rule of law (Ashworth 2002, 582).

Adam Crawford (2002, 122) notes that it is increasingly difficult to attract volunteers to participate in community panels and provide community input in restorative justice processes. As a result, representation on these panels may not be diverse and may even be unrepresentative of the community. This could lead to legitimacy problems. Lay people, who participate regularly, may be co-opted into "professional" values and lose touch with their communities.

Community Partnerships with Criminal Justice Agencies

To reduce victimization and allay fears of crime, some restorative and community justice initiatives revolve around creating community partnerships with criminal justice agencies. Community-oriented policing (COP) is an example of an effort to link citizens as individual members of the community to police operations and to establish a partnership between police and communities to reduce crime (Sampson 1999). Critics of COP in the restorative justice movement assert that community participation in COP has been limited to providing eyes and ears, political and monetary support to police, as well as statements expressing opposition to various forms of police misconduct. Little or no training for neighborhood members to assume a role in community policing has been provided. Thus, many restorative justice advocates believe community-oriented policing has not incorporated communities in a meaningful partnership (McCold and Wachtel 2002, 43).

More hope resides with problem-oriented policing (POP) in which community members help police identify and solve problems in their neighborhoods. Goldstein (1990) describes POP as police addressing community problems rather than focusing entirely on the administrative and organizational concerns. Instead, police should assume unconventional roles, as counselors, teachers, coaches, and so on, in response to specific contexts to address a specific community problem. For example, a police department might help the community set up an alternative recreation program for youth whose neighborhoods are afflicted by gang activity.

Various communities employ or are considering proposals to use problem-oriented policing. In Madison, Wisconsin, the police department has proposed to turn their traffic and narcotics teams into problem-oriented policing teams. The officers would be re-trained to target resources to specific problems. For instance, one team might address the problems of open-air drug dealing, while another team might devote time to solving burglaries and vehicle break-ins. They would like to provide more tailor-made responses to different parts of the city (Elbow 2003, 1A). In Oakland, California, a special problem-solving officer unit was designed to address blighted properties. The Beat Health Unit concentrates on cleaning up or closing down problem properties such as drug houses, liquor stores with loitering problems, and other blighted areas. Between 1988 and 2001, the unit successfully prosecuted 4,000 nuisance-abatement cases and was well-regarded among neighborhood watch groups (Harris and Martinez 2002). The Morena Valley Police in Riverside, California, expanded their problem-oriented policing program to also target blighted properties and to help probation officers deal with problem parolees (Gutierrez 1997, B01).

Circle sentencing also involves the community with criminal justice actors and agencies. Using consensus decision-making, participants speak out about the offense, starting with the victim's reactions. Eligible only to offenders who admit guilt and express regret, numerous actors become involved including judges, prosecutors, defense attorneys (in more serious cases), victims, offenders, service providers, support groups for victims and offenders, and other key community representatives. One of the goals of sentencing circles is to increase the community's efficacy in resolving disputes and preventing crime but also to aid in development of rehabilitative plans, address victim concerns and public safety issues (Bazemore 1998, 341).

Sentencing circles allow the community to recommend a sentence that is designed specifically for the offender and the crime committed. Recently, the Minnesota Supreme Court upheld this practice in Minnesota when a community sentencing circle recommended a sentence for a defendant charged with welfare fraud (Zack 2002, 2B). If the violator repaid the money and engaged in community service, the sentencing circle held, her record would be expunged. The sentence was controversial because the sentence recommendation went beyond the bounds of statutory law in Minnesota (Zack 2000, 3B). Still, the Minnesota Supreme Court upheld the sentence arguing that the legislation that authorized the use of sentencing circles in 1988 made a novel alternative process possible and provided a mechanism for allowing communities to meaningfully participate in the criminal justice process (Zack 2002, 2B). A similar concept was implemented in Gilroy, California which uses accountability boards to address juvenile offenses. The accountability boards, made up of Gilroy neighbors, hear cases involving first-time juvenile offenders, and recommend creative sentences designed to fit the offender and the crime. For example, a minor caught for graffiti might be required to re-paint the building or fence that was marred. A partnership formed with the San Jose Police Department, the Juvenile Justice Commission and the Juvenile Justice Coordinating Board facilitated this approach (Gardiner 1997).

Family group conferencing, community conferencing, and police conferencing usually involve close relatives to the victim and offender as well as police and social service providers. Oriented toward denouncing the crime but also supporting the offender, this set of processes focuses on offender reintegration and how the community can increase the odds of successful reintegration. The Central City Neighborhood Partnership in Minneapolis uses conferencing to improve quality of life in the downtown neighborhoods. In contrast to a police crackdown on crime, conferencing allows for a strengthening of community ties, a chance to reintegrate the offender and hold the offender accountable, and an opportunity for the community to uphold community standards without further harming the offender and simultaneously reducing community reliance on outside forces to reduce crime (Pranis n.d.).

Wisconsin has approximately twenty victim-offender conferencing programs, including both adults and juveniles. One of several projects—the Community Adolescent Program (CAP)—allows crime victims to interact with the youthful offender who committed the offense against them. In 2001, trained facilitators convened thirteen CAP victim-offender conferences. Victim participation is voluntary and the conference allows them to ask questions not normally addressed in court. Youth and their parents attend the conference. The youth offenders describe what they did and apologize. They often successfully participate in community service and restitution programs (Ingersoll 2002, B1).

Research findings on conferencing show that repeat criminal behavior, after conferencing, is one-third to one-half of that which is normally expected. Restitution agreements are reached in 95 percent of the cases and offenders report having greater empathy toward victims. Furthermore, families argue that in juvenile cases, their child's behavior changes after the conference experence. Often, parents stated that their family relationships with police officers improved as a result of conferencing (Van Ness and Strong 2002, 63; Paye 1999). These findings point to the building of social capital and greater social cohesion.

Community mediation (CM) programs involve the community in civil dispute resolution and the mechanisms employed range from formal adjudication to binding or nonbinding arbitration to mediation. CM programs receive cases from police, prosecutors, and probation or as voluntary walk-ins. Many criminal cases also are referred to CM, especially when they involve parties who maintain on-going relationships. Mediators do not impose decisions but facilitate negotiations and try to arrive at an agreement. CM programs have been used in divorce cases, child custody disputes, landlord-tenant disputes, labor disputes, and similar cases. CM can be transformative, forever changing the lives of victims and offenders (McCold 1999).

The Community Justice Center in Indianapolis, Indiana allows citizens to participate in community mediation. Most of the disputes are between neighbors (such as barking dogs, noisy vehicles, eyesores created by junky yards and so on). A negotiated agreement is found more than seventy percent of the time and in other communities with CM—such as Houston, Texas and Queens, New York—satisfaction levels reached eighty percent (Lucas 2003, 9; Busch 2002). In 2003, the Minnesota Association of Community Mediation celebrated twenty years of volunteer mediation service. With six programs, four in the Twin Cities and two others in Rochester and Northfield, they address neighbor disputes, some family issues, landlord-tenant disputes, and other similar cases. Unlike court, CM allows for a give-and-take discussion and provides convenient hours for clients, as CM is often available on weekends and evenings. Since

1993, the number of cases handled per year for CM providers has grown from 1,500 to over 4,000 in Minnesota with over 20,000 people served ("Community Mediation: 20 Years of Managing Conflicts" 2003, 14A).

Another restorative justice practice that entails extensive community involvement is reparative probation. In 1996, Vermont laypersons on reparative probation boards began to make sentencing decisions about the criminal offenders in their communities. Like other restorative justice processes, reparative probation requires offenders to admit guilt, to apologize to their victims and express remorse, and to make amends to the community. Although initially sentenced in court, the offenders may receive a suspended sentence upon completion of a reparative agreement (Clear and Cadora 2003, 82). Citizens who participate in reparative probation engage in problem-solving and build close ties to facilitate reintegration.

Winooski, Vermont became the twenty-sixth Vermont community to set up a reparative board. In Winooski, an offender is given the option by a police officer to appear before the reparative board. A judge then refers the case to a reparative board panel. Used to keep minor criminals out of a backlogged and overburdened court system, the program has been deemed effective, empowering to residents, and a cost savings measure ("Winooski Establishing Community Reparations Board" 2000). As of 1999, over eighty percent of 4,000 offenders in Vermont had successfully completed their reparative board restoration plans. Initial studies show that offenders who participate in the reparative process are less likely to re-offend than those who go through probation (Marks 1999).

Community courts also attempt to return a community to its normal state after a crime is committed. They may involve individual experiments undertaken by judges, an entire trial court system, or a state system of trial courts. They typically involve partnerships with the community to make a more formal judicial process accessible and visible. By reaching out to community-based organizations, they involve community residents in the process of dealing with the crime problems that concern them the most (Chase et al. 2000, 38–39). Started in 1993, Midtown Community Court in Manhattan has been credited with transforming a once-seedy area, inhabited by prostitutes and drug dealers, into an appealing business and residential district. It hears cases involving quality of life issues such as graffiti, drug dealing, and prostitution. Offenders, who are often arrested and arraigned on the same day, may be sent out wearing the Community Court blue vests to carry out community service. Viewed as a major success, Midtown's experiment has been used to develop community courts elsewhere (Brunswick 1998, 1A).

In the Sixth District of Washington, D.C., the Community Court handles criminal cases, usually drug possession and prostitution, in a nontraditional manner. Instead of an elongated trial, the defense attorney and the prosecutor confer to see how the defendant can be helped, what can be done to prevent future violations, and how the defendant can make restitution to the community. Typically, defendants do not plead. Rather, the charges stand until a court-ordered restoration plan is completed. The hope is that these types of courts can help turn around the lives of offenders who are afflicted by unemployment, drug addiction, homelessness, and so on (Santana 2002, A01). In 2001, Syracuse's North Side created a Community Court to address loitering, open container violations, and noise ordinance issues. Defendants appearing before the court are either fined or ordered to engage in community service to rectify the damage caused by the offense (Sieh 2003).

Bennett (1998) argues that community-based responses to crime can create safer communities. Often, community organizations are more effective than police in face-to-face contacts with those in their community. Particularly in areas where police are not trusted, community organizations can bridge the gap. Through participation in community organizations, solitary individuals can develop personas as public citizens and can act in their self-interest while also pursuing a collective good. Although community crime prevention programs have limitations, research indicates that when a sense of neighborhood identity exists, these neighbors can collaborate in forums to discuss common problems and then may be effective in creating better communities.

Community Restoration

Crime victims often experience loss of control and a sense of order in their lives. Many experience more than just material losses or physical pain or degradation. Their lives, once predictable, have been turned upside down. They need to know that what happened to them was wrong and that they were not responsible in some way for the harm suffered. Victims experience mental anguish and pain that goes far beyond the initial impact of the criminal offense. Accordingly, their need for order and control over their lives should be restored. Offenders also need to understand and appreciate the injuries inflicted on their victims and the community. Neither victims nor offenders can move forward without a healing process. Holding offenders accountable allows them to heal along with the victims (Zehr 1990).

Use of restorative justice techniques is aimed at not only restoring individual victims and offenders but the community as well. From a community's perspective, restorative justice means restoring a sense of peace and harmony or the feeling that justice has been served. Braithwaite (1998, 329) and other advocates of restorative justice believe that restoring peace and harmony without addressing injustice is insufficient. Although they recognize that restorative justice cannot solve persistent societal problems such as hunger and poverty, they assert that it should at a minimum not make these problems worse and that its remedies should always take into account these underlying structural injustices.

Critics question the broad goal of restoring communities. They ask, "exactly what is community restoration?" Generally, they contend that no agreed upon criteria exist on what methods should be used to restore communities or on how to calculate what amount of activity is adequate for restoration. Community service might be one way to achieve a degree of restoration but critics question whether community service can be done on a scale that truly rights the wrongs done to a community (Ashworth 2002, 583).

Braithwaite (2002, 66–69) argues that members of the community (beyond victims and offenders) who have been involved in restorative processes express high levels of satisfaction with their experiences. He notes that restorative justice successes have been modest and confined to microcommunity building in schools and families. However, he asserts that some of its effects may carry over into the macrocommunity as evidence increasingly shows that communities that exhibit strong social support experience less criminality.

Building Community Support for Restorative Justice

The National Institute of Corrections (2001) devised a facilitator guide for building community support for restorative justice practices. Kay Pranis and Peg Christian, major contributors to this guide, suggest processes that build community. These include creating or strengthening existing relationships, increasing community skills in problem solving, raising individual awareness and commitment to the common good, building the community's capacity to collectively deal with problems, and creating support systems for victims and offenders. Their nuts-and-bolts advice includes finding natural allies in the community who are interested in using new approaches to improve community safety and resolve conflicts within the community. They further suggest that advocates should turn to local institutions such as schools, businesses, social service providers, and others, that could provide valuable resources to the process of community building. They lay out a planning process such as how to define a community, how decisions will be made, the type of leadership structure, and individual responsibilities entailed and how to include participants in shared decision-making.

Kay Pranis argues that no firm blueprint exists for creating a restorative system; rather, the collaboration of stakeholders will determine what approaches will be used. State agencies could provide leadership in providing information on and articulating a vision of restorative justice. They could also provide much needed technical assistance, establish pilot programs, and provide feedback through program evaluations (Johnstone 2002, 158). Generally, restorative justice advocates argue that local communities should take greater responsibility for reducing crime and victimization and meet antisocial behaviors with a restorative response of reintegration and healing (Johnstone 2002, 154–156).

In conclusion, proponents of restorative justice believe that restorative justice processes generally build community and sustain community support by creating interlocking relationships, a strengthened community fabric, and preventing wear and tear on this fabric by fostering community involvement in response to crime.

References

Ashworth, Andrew. 2002. "Responsibilities, Rights and Restorative Justice." *British Journal of Criminology* 42: 578–595.

Barton, Charles. 2000. "Empowerment and Retribution in Criminal Justice." In *Restorative Justice: Philosophy to Practice*. Eds. Heather Strang and John Braithwaite. Burlington, VT: Ashgate Publishing, pp. 55–76.

Bazemore, Gordon. 1998. "The 'Community' in Community Justice: Issues, Themes, and Questions for the New Neighborhood Sanctioning Models." In *Community Justice: An Emerging Field*. Ed. David R. Karp. Lanham, MD: Rowman and Littlefield Publishers, Inc.

Bennett, Susan F. 1998. "Community Organizations and Crime." In *Community Justice: An Emerging Field*. Ed. David R. Karp. Lanham, MD: Rowman and Littlefield Publishers, Inc.

Braithwaite, John. 1998. "Restorative Justice." In *The Handbook of Crime and Punishment*. Ed. Michael Tonry. New York: Oxford University Press, pp. 323–244.

Braithwaite, John. 1999. "Symposium: A Future Where Punishment Is Marginalized: Realistic or Utopian?" *UCLA Law Review* 46 (August): 1727-1750.

Braithwaite, John. 2002. *Restorative Justice and Responsive Regulation.* Oxford: Oxford University Press.

Busch, Jennifer Thiele. 2002. "The Peacemakers." *Business and Management Practices* 44 (8): 44-47.

Brunswick, Mark. 1998. "Street Justice: Would It Work Here?" *Star Tribune* [Minneapolis] (April 14), p. 1A.

Cayley, David. 1998. *The Expanding Prison: The Crisis in Crime and Punishment and the Search for Alternatives.* Cleveland: Pilgrim Press.

Chase, Deborah J., Hon. Sue Alexander, and Hon. Barbara J. Miller. 2000. "Courts Responding to Communities: Community Courts and Family Law." *Journal of the Center for the Children & the Courts* 2: 37-54.

Christie, Nils. 1977. "Conflicts as Property." *British Journal of Criminology* 17: 1-15.

Clear, Todd R., and Eric Cadora, with Sarah Bryer and Charles Swartz. 2003. *Community Justice.* Belmont, CA: Wadsworth/Thomson Learning.

Cnaan, Ram A., with Robert Je. Wineburg and Stephanie C. Boddie. 1999. *The Newer Deal: Social Work and Religion in Partnership.* New York: Columbia University Press.

"Community Mediation; 20 Years of Managing Conflicts." 2003. *Star Tribune* [Minnesota] (January 3), p. 14A.

Crawford, Adam. 2002. "The State. Community and Restorative Justice: Heresy, Nostalgia and Butterfly Collecting." In *Restorative Justice and the Law.* Ed. Lode Walgrave. Portland, OR: Willan Publishing, pp. 101-129.

Elbow, Steven. 2003. "Cops Plan Revamp to Tackle Problems." *Capital Times* [Madison, WI] (March 27), p. 1A.

Gardiner, Lisa. 1997. "Citizens Have Say in Youth Sentencing in Gilroy, California." *The Dispatch* [Gilroy, CA] (October 23). <http://web.lexis-nexis.com/universe> (accessed August 12, 2003).

Glazer, Sarah. 2001. "Faith-Based Initiatives: Is U.S. Funding of Religious Groups Constitutional?" *CQ Researcher* 11:17, May 4, 2001): 377-400.

Goldstein, Herman. 1990. *Problem-Oriented Policing.* Philadelphia: Temple University Press.

Gutierrez, Joe. 1997. "Police Get OK to Expand Police Program." *Press Enterprise* [Riverside, CA] (December 3), p. B01.

Harris, Harry, and Mike Martinez. 2002. "City's Problem Property Cops Back on the Job." *Oakland Tribune* [Oakland, CA] (December 5). <http://web.lexis-nexis.com/universe> (accessed August 12, 2003).

Hope, Tim. 1995. "Community Crime Prevention." In *Building A Safer Society: Strategic Approaches to Crime Prevention: Crime and Justice: A Review of Research, Volume 19*. Eds. Michael Tonry and David P. Farrington. Chicago: University of Chicago Press, 21–89.

Ingersoll, Brenda. 2002. "Meeting Their Victims Affects Young Offenders; The Results Can Be Impressive, As the Kids Put a Face to the Victim, and Sometimes They Apologize." *Wisconsin State Journal* (October 7), p. B1.

Johnstone, Gerry. 2002. *Restorative Justice: Ideas, Values, Debates*. Portland, OR: Willan Publishing.

Kurki, Leena. 2000. "Restorative and Community Justice in the United States." *Crime and Justice* 27: 235–291.

Marks, Alexandra. 1999. "Instead of Jail, Criminals Face Victims." *Christian Science Monitor* (September 8). < http://search.csmonitor.com/durable/1999/09/08/p1s3.htm > (accessed August 12, 2003).

McCold, Paul, "Restorative Justice Practice—The State of the Field 1999." < http://www.realjustice.org/Pages/v199papers/vt_mccold.htm > (accessed August 12, 2003).

McCold, Paul and Benjamin Wachtel. 2002. "Community Is Not a Place: A New Look at Community Justice Initiatives." In *Repairing Communities Through Restorative Justice*. Ed. John G. Perry. Lanham, MD: American Correctional Association, pp. 39–53.

McHugh, Gerald Austin. 1978. *Christian Faith and Criminal Justice: Toward a Christian Response to Crime and Punishment*. New York: Paulist Press.

McKelvey, Blake. 1977. *American Prisons: A History of Good Intentions*. Montclair, NJ: Patterson Smith.

Moore, Mark H. 1999. "Security and Community Development." In *Urban Problems and Community Development*. Eds. Ronald F. Ferguson and William T. Dickens. Washington, D.C.: Brookings Institution Press, pp. 293–337.

Morris, Allison, and Gabrielle Maxwell. 2001. "Restorative Conferencing." In *Restorative Justice Community: Repairing Harm and Transforming Communities*. Eds. Gordon Bazemore and Mara Schiff. Cincinnati: Anderson Publishing, pp. 173–197.

Morris, Allison, and Warren Young. 2000. "Reforming Criminal Justice: The Potential of Restorative Justice." In *Restorative Justice: Philosophy to Practice*. Eds. Heather Strang and John Braithwaite. Burlington, VT: Ashgate Publishing, pp. 11–31.

National Institute of Corrections. 2001. "Restorative Justice: Principles, Practices and Implementation—Section 4: Building Community and Resource Capacity." Washington, D.C.: National Institute of Corrections.

Paye, Amanda L. 1999. "Comment: Communities Take Control of Crime: Incorporating the Conferencing Model into the United States Juvenile Justice System." *Pacific Rim Law and Policy Journal* 8 (January): 161–187.

Pranis, Kay. "Conferencing and the Community." < http://www.realjustice.org/Pages/mn98papers/nacc_pra.htm > (accessed August 12, 2003).

Roach, Kent. 2000. "Changing Punishment at the Turn of the Century: Restorative Justice on the Rise." *Canadian Journal of Criminology* 42 (July): 249–280.

Sampson, Robert J. 1999. "Security and Community Development." In *Urban Problems and Community Development*. Eds. Ronald F. Ferguson and William T. Dickens. Washington, D.C.: Brookings Institution Press, pp. 241–292.

Santana, Authur. 2002. "D.C. Court Tries Problem Solving; In Misdemeanors, Behavioral Advice Could Replace Jail Time." *Washington Post* (December 2), p. A1.

Sieh, Maureen. 2003. "Community Court Takes Violations Seriously; Judge Says the Cases That Are Dismissed Are Legally Insufficient." *The Post-Standard* [Syracuse, NY] (July 24). < http://web.lexis-nexis.com/universe > (accessed August 12, 2003).

Umbreit, Mark S.; Robert B. Coates and Betty Vos. 2002. "The Impact of Restorative Justice Conferencing: A Review of 63 Empirical Studies in 5 Countries." St. Paul, MN: Center for Restorative Justice & Peacemaking.

Van Ness, Daniel W., and Karen Heetderks Strong. 2002. *Restoring Justice*. 2d ed. Cincinnati: Anderson Publishing.

Wachtel, Ted, and Paul McCold. 2001. "Restorative Justice in Everyday Life." In *Restorative Justice and Civil Society*. Eds. Heather Strang and John Braithwaite. Cambridge: Cambridge University Press, pp. 114–129.

"Winooski Establishing Community Reparations Board." 2000. Associated Press State & Local Wire. (March 7). < http://web. lexis-nexis.com/universe > (accessed August 12, 2003).

Zack, Margaret. 2000. "Appeals Court Limits Reach of Justice Programs." *Star Tribune* [Minneapolis] (May 3), p. 3B.

Zack, Margaret. 2002. "High Court Affirms Sentencing Circle; Communities Deserve A Say, Justice Writes." *Star Tribune* [Minneapolis] (January 18), p. 2B.

Zehr, Howard. 1990. *Changing Lenses: A New Focus for Crime and Justice*. Scottsdale, PA: Herald Press.

CHAPTER 6

Restorative Justice and Corrections

Restorative Justice and the Multiple Goals of Corrections

With the many, often conflicting, goals of corrections and punishment such as deterrence, retribution, incapacitation and rehabilitation and in some instances, restorative justice, development of a unified correctional philosophy and approach to punishment is highly unlikely and may not even be desirable. As any approach by itself is fallible, some argue that multiple and conflicting goals create a checks and balances system that protects society against excess and error. Society has contradictory attitudes toward crime, in part engendered by the conflicting goals of corrections and punishment (Roach 2000, 251).

Restorative justice as a correctional tool has three faces: retributive accountability, rehabilitative healing and deterrent crime prevention. Because proponents of restorative justice are not unified behind one of these approaches, it can be used for very different purposes (Roach 2000, 263–264). Proponents of retributive accountability say that offenders should accept responsibility for their actions, that short-term incarceration is not sufficient by itself, and that offenders should acknowledge how their crimes affected victims and society. For those who find retributive theories compelling, this is the most appealing "face" of restorative justice. (Roach 264–265). Advocates of rehabilitative healing also find comfort in restorative justice. Restorative justice is portrayed as treatment and healing-oriented not only for the offender but also for the victim and the community. Finally, defenders of restorative justice argue that it is the most effective way to prevent crime. Offenders who have been reintegrated into their community are are less likely to re-offend. Accordingly, they claim that restorative justice programs operate as a mechanism for deterrent crime prevention (Roach 2000, 266–267).

This chapter will examine the three faces of restorative justice as well as the effects this tripartite philosophy have on corrections in the United States. First, it is important to look at the evolution of community-based corrections in the U.S.

Traditional Community-Based Corrections

Community-based corrections refers to sanctions that lawbreakers serve in the community other than serving time in prisons or jails. Probation and parole are perhaps the oldest and most common community-based sanctions. Today, several community-based correction options are used including intensive supervision, restitution, community service, work release, electronic monitoring, and so on. This expanded emphasis on community corrections emerged in the United States in the 1980s and 1990s. As part of the rehabilitation and treatment strategies fostered in the 1970s, community corrections were seen as less stigmatizing and more humane than prisons (Kurki 2000, 260).

Even so, community corrections in the 1970s were underfunded, understaffed, and poorly administered—much as they remain today. Consequently, many community corrections programs are and have been judged as ineffective. Instead of being oriented toward rehabilitation orientation, today's community-based corrections are used for supervising offenders to ensure that they do not break the law and to punish them if they do (Dean-Myrda and Cullen 1998). The shift from a rehabilitative perspective to a tough-on-crime approach did not lead to a reduction in recidivism. Instead, community-based sanctions became a mechanism for re-incarcerating offenders for minor technical violations of their intermediate sanctions (Tonry 1998b).

In the mid-to-late 1990s and the early part of the twenty-first century, some evidence suggests that the pendulum is swinging back to using community-based corrections to rehabilitate and reintegrate offenders into the community (Kurki 2000, 262). Ranging from treatment services, job placement services, and neighborhood interventions to early intervention, community involvement in crime prevention and reparative community service projects, community justice, and restorative justice principles are being integrated into correctional systems across the United States (Kurki 2000, 263).

Restorative Justice and Community-Based Corrections

A number of community correctional practitioners embrace restorative justice as a means for implementing community-based corrections. Primarily, they tap into the rehabilitative healing and crime prevention aspects of restorative justice.

This model of corrections is supported by a public safety rubric that combines healing victims, offenders, and communities with the inculcation of guardians who form a buffer between vulnerable community targets and potential offenders. Three states—Washington, Vermont, and Wisconsin—have taken steps in this direction (Smith 2001, 2). If this broader perspective is accepted in other state and local communities, various restorative justice community corrections techniques could be successfully implemented.

Traditional Community-Based Corrections Revamped with a Restorative Focus

The following traditional community-based corrections tools can be revamped to serve a restorative justice purpose. Probation and parole, electronic monitoring and home confinement, work release, restitution, and community service already have some restorative elements. Using them for restorative justice purposes might transform them into more effective tools.

Probation and Parole

With more than 4.5 million adults on probation and parole, these mechanism are the primary alternatives to incarceration in the United States (Waters 2003). Probation first garnered attention in the early twentieth century and was widely accepted by 1920. It allows offenders to live in communities while under state supervision. Offenders placed on probation or released on parole must abide by certain conditions and rules. For example, an offender on probation may be required to go to drug counseling, pay restitution, keep a job, report periodically to a probation officer, and so on. Violation of any of the rules or conditions could result in revocation of either probation. According to MacKenzie et al. (1999), probation reduces criminal activity and the re-offend rate among certain types of crime categories.

Parole involves early release from prison after a portion of the sentence is served. Nearly 600,000 offenders are released on parole each year (Jones 2003). This release is conditional on continued good behavior by the released inmate—meaning the commission of any new crimes could return the newly-released inmate back to prison.

Many have argued that probation and parole should be "reinvented." Some advocate enhanced supervision of probationers and parolees by tightening up rule setting, detecting of rule violations, and carrying out sanctions (Kleiman 1999, 1920). This approach could satisfy those who are concerned primarily with public safety. Others reject this approach, claiming that unless communities are restored, reinventing probation and parole in this manner leads to more revocations, more arrests and longer prison terms—thus widening the net of social control with nonrestorative effects (Roach 2000, 260).

Some promote "broken window" probation which combines the reintegrative and the public safety approaches. Studies show that half of probationers do not comply with their conditional release rules and a large number lose contact with their probation officer. Advocates of the broken window approach claim public safety comes first and argue for supervision in the neighborhood, rather than through scheduled office visits. They assert that probation avoiders should be forced to adhere to the terms and conditions of probation and that law enforcement and probation officers should work together for this purpose. More supervision of those at risk for violation of their conditions should occur. Like those concerned about reintegration, this approach sponsors community partnerships in which offenders have access to social services ("Broken Window" Probation: The Next Step in Fighting Crime 1999). Although this approach expresses some concern for rehabilitative healing, its main focus is crime prevention through deterrence.

The typical prisoner released on parole is more likely to have been convicted of a drug offense, will have served an average of 27 months in prison, has the equivalent of an eleventh grade education, will be released into central cities of a metropolitan area, and has few skills for purposes of reintegration into the community (Travis and Petersilia 2001). To avoid destabilization of these communities and to make probation and parole restorative, reintegration of offenders into communities must become the primary goal, not just monitoring them for purposes of revocation. Todd Clear, Dina Rose, and Judith Ryder (2001) make the following recommendations:

1. Direct social services to families while offenders are incarcerated by providing short-term financial assistance, mental health assistance, parenting classes, and day care and adult mentors for children.
2. Help maintain family bonds through family contact with incarcerated offenders by providing transportation to prison and low-cost telephone service between inmates and families.
3. Ensure stable environments for children of inmates through counseling and early intervention programs.
4. Establish prerelease transition plans that maximize family health by determining: whether inmates should return to their families immediately upon release, whether they should return to their communities or move to new neighborhoods, and whether families and released inmates should move to new neighborhoods together.
5. Connect prerelease inmates to social services, employment and housing options, counseling to address inmate reentry fears, and how to cope with uniting with family.
6. Provide transitional housing for inmates and access to a service or assessment center that helps recent inmates obtain identification papers, clothing, employment, and so on.
7. Help ex-offenders become self-sufficient by providing employment assistance through education programs and encouraging the hiring of ex-offenders.

8. Reduce financial costs on ex-offenders in the initial release period by reducing or eliminating supervision fees, providing short-term assistance such as paying the first month's rent for an apartment, and starting up utilities in a home.
9. Make low-cost drug treatment programs available to offenders.
10. Help ex-offenders make community connections such as self-help groups, links to community mentors, and links to neighborhood projects.
11. Develop programs that help ex-offenders overcome the stigma associated with incarceration by educating the community and by assisting them as they reintegrate.

Project Safeway in Chicago, Illinois is a community-based probation center that forges partnerships among the Adult Probation Department, nonprofit service providers, and the community. This program offers a variety of offender programs such as an orientation preparing offenders for reentry into the community, local community college G.E.D. instruction, Treatment Alternatives to Special Clients for substance abuse, job training and job placement services, and parenting and health education. Although not completely fulfilling the recommendations (listed above) made by Clear et al., Project Safeway makes giant strides toward a community model that may reduce recidivism and prevent community deterioration (Leaf, Lurigio, and Martin 1998).

Ideally, probationers and parolees would be less likely to re-offend or break conditional release rules and regulations if a social support network existed for them. Others add that limiting the state's ability to revoke liberty of those who fail to meet reentry conditions would enhance the success of probation and parole and make reintegration a more prominent goal (Travis and Petersilia 2001; Petersilia 2001).

Although all states have some sort of prerelease program, they differ in accessibility and restrictions. Most states do not have formal prerelease centers or programs that facilitate the goal of reintegration. In most states, inmates are released from the halfway houses or minimum custody facilities without any reentry process (Austin 2001, 314–315). For those inmates who are in a reentry program they have access to education, job training, substance abuse counseling, and social network resources in the community from other state, local, and private agencies (Austin 2001, 317). Only a few states provide housing assistance upon release. Participation in these programs usually starts just a few weeks prior to release. Inmates usually receive a nominal amount of financial assistance that ranges from $25 to $200 plus clothing and bus fare to some location within the state. Washington State is the most active in prerelease activities, providing thirty to forty percent of inmates access to a prerelease center. Corrections officers also engage in early release planning; two years before release they initiate a release plan for each inmate. When it comes to prerelease planning, however, Washington is the exception, rather than the rule. There is great disparity in inmate accessibility to prerelease and reintegration programs from state to state (Austin 2001, 320).

Electronic Monitoring and Home Confinement

Electronic monitoring and home confinement technology may enhance the success of probation and parole programs. Home confinement technology which emerged in the form of a home-monitoring unit and a transmitter worn by the offender in the late 1970s is used as part of a number of programs that supervise convicted offenders in the community ("Offender Supervision with Electronic Technology" 2003). In 1988, only 2,300 offenders were subject to electronic supervision in the U.S. By January 1998, 1,500 house arrest electronic monitoring programs were in place, with 95,000 electronic monitoring units in use ("Keeping Track of Electronic Monitoring" 1999). As of 2003, the exact number of those being electronically supervised is unknown.

Originally established to reduce correctional costs, electronic monitoring and home confinement programs may serve other purposes. Several benefits, from a restorative justice perspective, are derived from electronic supervision of offenders. First, electronic monitoring and home confinement may allow offenders to reintegrate into communities by giving them the opportunity to take advantage of rehabilitative services. Second, electronic monitoring may lead to greater compliance with reintegration plans that incorporate treatment (Finn and Steves 2002; Martin 2003). Although home confinement is not the same as incarceration, it provides a measure of community protection that surpasses unsupervised release. It may deter offenders from departing from their conditions of release as violations can be easily detected (McCarthy and McCarthy, Jr. 1997, 213).

Some negative effects are associated with electronic monitoring and home confinement. Offenders, who are homebound except for release time for work, school, religious services, and treatment, become bored. They may take their immobility out on their family members, increasing tensions at home (McCarthy and McCarthy, Jr. 1997, 213). The offender's dependence on family for obtaining everyday essentials, such as shopping for groceries, picking up the laundry, and running errands, puts pressure on other family members and increases the offender's resentment level. In addition, the monitoring bracelet that they must wear can be humiliating, making them self-conscious about their diminished status (McCarthy and McCarthy, Jr. 1997, 218).

Although not correlated with reductions in recidivism, electronic supervision technology makes community-based corrections through treatment, counseling, and so on, more viable. As such, its use is appealing to those who endorse the rehabilitative healing component of restorative justice.

Work Release

Since the 1920s, correctional officials have tried to address the inadequate job training and lack of marketable skills of prisoners through work release programs. The idea did not fully catch on until 1955. By 1972, every state had a work release program in place except Mississippi and Nevada (Skorackyj 2000). Mississippi has a work release program in place now.

Under work release programs, select prisoners, who are at the end of their prison terms work in the community and return to confinement during their nonworking hours. Work release programs were seen by reformers as a way to help inmates begin reintegrating in the community by giving them legitimate employment opportunities (Turner and Petersilia 1996). Work release also allows prisoners to earn income, pay back the state for part of the costs of incarceration, possibly contribute to victim restitution, develop some savings for their eventual release, and learn positive work habits (Phelan 1997).

An evaluation of Washington state's work release programs shows positive results. Nearly 25 percent of all prisoners released in Washington were successfully reintegrated to the community through work release. These programs enabled the prisoners to attain gainful employment, re-develop ties to the community, pay for part of their confinement costs, and remain mostly drug free (Turner and Petersilia 1998). Although the evaluation of Washington state's work release program reveals that these programs do not reduce recidivism rates or correctional costs, it offers hope to those who advocate rehabilitative healing as part of restorative justice, as most believe that work release helps inmates reintegrate into the community. Work release, if more widely used, could be an important component of a restorative justice approach.

Restitution

All fifty states in the U.S. have statutory provisions for victim restitution. Restitution is the requirement that the offender, as a condition of probation, repair the harm inflicted on the victim by the crime committed. Usually restitution is ordered for property offenses. (Davis and Bannister 1995). Yet many barriers to enforcement exist, such as failures to carry out judicial orders, using restitution to cover other costs such as court costs, fees, and costs of incarceration and inadequate coordination among agencies who collect and disburse victim restitution monies ("The Importance of Restitution" 2000).

Restitution orders may hold offenders accountable for their crimes and provide victims with some monetary compensation to cover their losses. This form of corrections in the community is important to the retributive accountability branch of restorative justice. From this perspective, the restitution payments should remind offenders of the direct harm they inflicted on their victims and their communities. Although restitution payments from offenders to victims can never fully compensate them for the harm done, it signals an effort on the part of offenders to right their wrongs. Restitution is often therapeutic for offenders, in that they actively participate in a sanction that seeks to make amends instead of passively being punished in jail or prison (Bakker 1994, 1498-1499). Repairing harm and holding the offender accountable to the community are fundamental principles underlying restorative justice and community-based corrections (Turpin 1999).

Community Service

Doing work for the benefit of the community is part of community restoration, since it can mean literally making the community whole again. Sometimes referred to as symbolic restitution, the work done benefits the entire community rather than just an individual victim. Community service usually requires offenders to perform a specified number of hours of public service work. Generally, in the United States, community service is levied on offenders whose offenses do not have a direct victim—for example, those with a drunk-driving conviction. In the U.S., community service began as part of probation in 1966. The successful operation of community service programs requires determinations on what type of work will be performed, who will be eligible to perform it, and who will reap its benefits (Etter and Hammond 2001).

By providing a service to the community, such as helping to clean up graffiti or engaging in roadside trash collection, inmates are held accountable for their offenses, do not have to go to jail, and are not levied fines, restitution payments, or forfeitures that they cannot afford. Even with these benefits, community service has been plagued with concerns that this is not "real" punishment, that offenders do not necessarily learn their lesson, and that holding them accountable for their hours of service places demands on already overworked personnel (Mays and Winfree 2002, 263).

Research on the success or failure of community service programs is scarce. An evaluation of the Vera Institute's community service project in New York concluded that recidivism rates did not go down, that prison diversion goals were met and that the program saved money (Tonry 1998a, 89–90). Advocates of restorative justice who have a crime-prevention focus argue that offenders should become involved in programs that decrease the likelihood of recidivism. Despite early research that indicates that community service may not reduce recidivism, a number of scholars still recommend it as a means of sanctioning the offender and restoring the community. The program developed by the Kansas Department of Corrections has reported a high degree of completion and has been effective in successfully reintegrating offenders back into the community (Etter and Hammond 2001). Repairing harm to the community and restoring offenders serves two major goals of restorative justice.

Restorative Justice Techniques with Correctional Implications

Victim-offender reconciliation efforts, sentencing circles, and reparative boards were described in detail in chapter 3. The correctional implications of these restorative justice techniques, as well as those of reintegrative shaming, will be explored in the current section.

Victim-Offender Reconciliation Efforts

Efforts at victim-offender reconciliation may take the form of victim-offender panels, victim-offender mediation, or conferencing. In victim-offender panels (VOPs), a discussion occurs between a panel of victims and offenders who did not participate in the particular offenses against these victims. VOPs give the victims an opportunity to explain how the offenses affected their lives. It is not always possible for victims and the offenders responsible for their harm to meet directly. For example a rape victim could be too traumatized to face the offender. In other cases, an offender may not have been identified and therefore not available to participate in reconciliation efforts. Victim-offender panels have shown the most success in cases involving victims of drunk drivers and victims of burglary. Reconciliation may help change the anti-social attitudes and behaviors of offenders as they are confronted with the damage they have inflicted (Braswell, Fuller and Lozoff 2001, 149).

In victim-offender mediation (VOM), victims meet with their offenders and, with the assistance of a mediator, discuss their perceptions of the offense and what steps offenders could take to make amends (Bright 1997; Hughes and Mossman 2002, 96; Taylor 1996). Evaluations of VOM used in juvenile proceedings indicate that victims and offenders who participate voluntarily experience high levels of satisfaction. Over ninety percent of mediation sessions resulted in negotiated restitution plans to compensate victims and more than eighty percent of offenders met their restitution obligations. Victims felt less fear and anxiety after participating in VOM (Umbreit 1994). According to some research, offenders were less likely to re-offend if they participated in VOM programs (Arrigo and Schehr 1998). Young offenders in particular commit fewer additional crimes within a one-year follow-up period. In addition, these offenders' self-esteem is enhanced, as they have the opportunity to engage in productive, constructive work (Cunha 1999). Other research indicates that VOM offenders, compared to offenders who did not participate in victim offender reconciliation, were incarcerated for shorter periods of time, time served was in jails rather than prisons, and counties were saved substantial amounts of money (Coates and Gehm 1985).

Like VOM, conferencing—often referred to as family group conferencing—involves the victim and offender in discussions about the crime and its effects on the victim's life. However, conferencing broadens the conversation to include families, community support groups, social welfare agents, attorneys, and police. Other actors are included in the conversation to give offenders a sense that others in the community care for them and to enhance the sense of accountability that offenders feel toward their family and community (Bright 1997). Agreements are reached through conferencing that allow all affected parties to have input, express concerns, and, hopefully, forge ties between the parties and the community that will provide offenders a network of social support. Given that outcomes are established by a group of people who also were affected by the crime, offenders are more likely to accept responsibility for their actions and take steps to restore the community (Paye 1999, 184).

A pilot VOM program in Howard County, Maryland focuses primarily on property crimes and misdemeanors. Before victims and offenders are brought together, they are screened to make sure that offenders are willing to make amends. One elderly couple whose home had been burglarized was unable to sleep at night as they wondered why they were singled out. Later, during VOM, they found out that it was a random act and were able to regain peace of mind. They were satisfied that the offender was genuinely sorry for his actions and that he was headed toward reintegration into the community (Surkiewicz 2002).

Little research has been conducted on conferencing in the United States. Studies In New Zealand, however, show that conferencing has worked well with young offenders by reducing the number of juvenile cases processed in court, by increasing offender accountability, and by saving costs. Families, offenders, and victims express a high degree of satisfaction with conferencing (Cunha 1999). In the studies completed in the U.S., about ninety percent of juvenile offenders who participated in conferencing indicated that the conference agreement was fair while 95 percent of victims believed the outcome was fair. Over ninety percent of victims and offenders in a Bethlehem, Pennsylvania study and a Minnesota study recommended participation in conferencing to others (Umbreit, Coates and Voss 2002). Youth who had not participated in conferencing were much more likely to re-offend (Hines 2000).

Various concerns about victim reconciliation programs include their net widening effects as offenders who might have been released come under state supervision, sentence disparities levied under private justice, inadequate punishment, and undue pressures to engage in mediation rather than facing the consequences of the traditional justice system (Lucas 2001). Still, victim reconciliation efforts appeal to those who value retributive accountability. Offenders who take responsibility for their actions and truly regret the harm they have caused may be able to reintegrate into society more successfully. To the degree that offenders are less likely to offend, another goal—deterrent crime prevention—is met.

Sentencing Circles

Borrowing from Native American peacemaking ceremonies, sentencing circles take many forms and are described by different names, such as "circles of understanding," "healing circles," "support circles" and "agreement circles." Usually offenders petition to have a council or community justice committee consider their circumstances. If accepted into a circle, offenders are present throughout the circle meeting. Numerous others participate, including experienced circle-keepers, representatives from the formal justice system, and community members. Although sentencing may occur, many of the circles become support circles or follow-up circles that monitor the fulfillment of agreements (Coates, Umbreit and Vos 2000).

During a circle meeting, victims and offenders share their stories. Support systems for both victims and offenders are created. Support circles exist for victims, helping them come to terms with their victimization, and for offenders, helping them gain an understanding of how their offense affected other parties, to take responsibility for their actions, and to take positive steps by giving evidence of sincere remorse. Eventually, as circles evolve to serve the purpose of healing, then the offender healing circle will identify elements that should be part of a sentencing plan. The sentencing circle, headed by a judge, ultimately must reach a consensus on a sentencing plan and the judge approves the sentence. In follow-up meetings, the offenders return to the circle to give them a status report on their progress. If insufficient progress is made, offenders may be sent back to court for traditional justice system sanctions (Ulrich 1999, 439).

Little research has been conducted on the effectiveness of circles. Most research looks at participant satisfaction and does not address whether circles reduce recidivism. Most studies agree, however, that circles offer good resources for helping offenders transition back into society. Re-entry or follow-up circles have potential that has not been fully realized. In the studies, there is little agreement about the types of cases that are most appropriate for circles. Some advocate the use of circles only in cases where offenders show remorse, in cases involving nonviolent offenders, or in cases where the community is the victim and no direct victim exists (Coates, Umbreit and Vost 2000).

Reparative Boards

Community reparative boards, such as those used in Vermont, consist of a small group of citizens who are trained for the purpose of conducting public face-to-face meetings with offenders as offenders discuss the negative consequences of their crimes. Reparative boards deal primarily with nonviolent and minor offenses after a court has sentenced convicted offenders to participate in this process. Board members, after meeting with offenders and all the parties involved, recommend a set of sanctions and, if the parties agree, a proposed time line for completing the measures is set. Usually, after monitoring the offender's progress for ninety days, the board submits a report to the court documenting the extent to which the offender has complied with the sanctions (McCarney 2001, 9).

In the United States, Vermont's program is unique because it is the only one of its kind that operates at the state level. With 62 active community reparative boards in operation, this program is supported by courts, prosecutors, defense attorneys, and communities. These community boards take part in sentencing of nonviolent offenders, with offenders meeting with the boards between two and three times (Dzur and Wertheimer 2002). This approach has resulted in a slightly lower recidivism rate than conventional probation (Hansen 1997). One of the goals of reparative boards is to help offenders reintegrate by helping them understand their role as a citizen in the community and finding ways to prevent re-offending. In exchange for offenders making amends to the victims and to the community, the community also must offer reintegration. However, board members are afflicted by philosophical disagreements about the offender contract and whether it should be more punitive or more rehabilitative in nature (Karp 2002). Still others defend reparative boards as more humanizing than traditional criminal justice processes and as more beneficial to the community (Hansen 1997).

Reintegrative Shaming

Reintegrative shaming is based on the showing of disapproval for offenders' actions while maintaining respect for offenders as human beings. Ultimately, reintegrative shaming relies on forgiveness and allows offenders to rejoin the community as productive citizens (Braithwaite

2002, 74). Furthermore, the theory behind reintegrative shaming holds that societies are forgiving and respectful, while also allowing for a community expression of disapproval for bad acts. According to this theory, societies that use reintegrative shaming should have lower crime rates (Braithwaite 2000). Internal controls—meaning cultural restraints and social structures—are more effective in lowering crime rates than external controls such as prisons and harsh penalties (Van Ness and Strong 2002, 107). Shaming is reintegrative when it reinforces offenders' ties to community as law-abiding citizens and maintains respect for the offenders while directing condemnation toward the bad act (Hay 2001).

Whereas the punishments handed out in the judicial system divide offender and punisher by turning the relationship into one based merely on infliction of injury, reintegrative shaming builds ties between and among the affected parties and may be potentially restorative for all. The traditional criminal justice system typically results in a situation in which offenders on trial feel little shame and are not encouraged to take responsibility for their actions. Perversely, offenders may become owners of their crimes, feeling pride and accomplishment as a result of society's efforts to stigmatize their offenses. The trial and plea bargain processes are more likely to make victims feel shame than offenders (Braswell, Fuller, and Lozoff 2001, 150). The traditional criminal justice system is frequently ineffectual from both victim and offender standpoints. Its results are often less than satisfactory and some attribute this to its inability to effectively incorporate shame in a reintegrative fashion.

Before forgiveness can be attained, select offenders are invited to take part in a restorative conference which consists of offenders, members of offenders' families, victims, members of victims' families, and other supporters along with a trained restorative justice facilitator. According to Gerry Johnstone (2002, 115–116), these conferences attempt to:

1. get offenders to recognize the consequences of their actions;
2. help offenders understand lifestyle issues that led them to offend;
3. identify ways to alter their lifestyles so that re-offending is less likely;
4. move them to apologize and make restitution to their victims;
5. allow victims to tell their stories and explain how the offenses affected them, and
6. encourage victims to move toward forgiveness of their offenders. Shaming ceremonies should be used to reconcile the offender with the community and therefore should be followed by forgiveness to result in true reintegration of the offender into the community (Johnstone 2002,121). Arguably, if shame is acknowledged, and is followed by remorse and apology, victims may be encouraged to regain self-esteem and a sense of self-respect and may also be more ready to forgive their offenders (McDonald and Moore 2001, 135).

Opponents of reintegrative shaming believe that government should not involve itself in the degradation that accompanies shaming penalties. Civil libertarians contend that shaming, whether reintegrative or stigmatizing, is humiliating and not geared toward rehabilitation ("Developments in Law: Alternatives to Incarceration" 1998, 1972–1973). Furthermore, they argue that shaming may produce more criminality through the labeling effect (labeling offenders as criminals and not worthy of reintegration). Shaming penalties may work only in those instances in which offenders still care about what their community thinks of them (Shatzkin 1998, A20). Shaming penalties can result in self-destruction. A few incidences of suicide have been linked to shame sentences. Shame may make re-entry into society more difficult by imposing unwarranted hardships on the shamed offender. If shaming ceremonies became everyday, routine occurrences, the public might start ignoring them which could lead to a diminishing of their deterrent effects (Massaro 1991, 1931-1932).

Proponents see shaming ceremonies as an alternative to incarceration and an effective restraint on crime (McMurry 1997, 12-14). Others argue that if used as a reintegrative tool, shame could be an efficient, fiscally sound, and positive means to deter crime and reduce recidivism. Unlike other alternatives to incarceration, shaming allows the expression of moral outrage (Book 1999). Furthermore, shaming avoids the afflictive aspects of imprisonment. Incarcerated offenders, especially first-time offenders, are more likely to become hardened criminals as they learn by example from other prisoners. Prisons, then, can turn into training grounds on how to become a better criminal. Those who are imprisoned have difficulties when trying to reintegrate into society (Kahan 1996).

From Braithwaite's perspective (1989), reintegrative shaming is an irreplaceable tool. Shaming should not be used to stigmatize but should instead be combined with efforts to reintegrate offenders into society. Penalties alone, according to reintegrative shaming theory, are insufficient because they do not allow society to discourage offensive behavior through outright condemnation.

Reintegrative shaming, combined with the philosophy of restorative justice, allows society to recognize the offender's worth as a human being but disapprove of the wrongdoing. It rejects scolding and lecturing and instead tries to engender empathy for all parties. Rather than being passive observers, offenders are actively involved in taking responsibility for their actions. Negative incidents, such as crime, may become learning opportunities in which communities learn to deal with wrongdoing and conflict in a constructive manner by building empathy, developing a sense of community and reducing the likelihood of re-offending (Wachtel and McCold 2001).

Since reintegrative shaming is most likely to be effective in "close-knit" societies, the social conditions in the United States may not be very conducive to reintegrative shaming, particularly in larger urban areas. A communitarian society, a sense of interdependenc, and a strong family system enhance the effectiveness of shaming ceremonies while unemployment, dissolution of family ties, and cultural diversity may weaken a sense of interdependency and undermine the effective use of reintegrative shaming (Massaro 1991; Massaro 1997).

While little data exists to illustrate the effectiveness of shaming in deterring crime or reducing recidivism, a lot of data exists to illustrate the failure of the traditional criminal justice disposition processes. Research suggests that prison stays of more than two years are counterproductive, lead to dissolution of families and community ties, and ultimately result in recidivism (Viano 2000; Rottman and Casey 2000; Duguid 2000). Advocates of shaming believe that sentencing nonviolent offenders to prison is outmoded and only makes them more hardened criminals when they are released (Etzioni 1999).

Although some scholars believe reintegrative shaming is not practical, they still embrace shaming penalties. Shaming penalties, used continuously and linked to an offender's reformed behavior and compliance with a rehabilitative plan, may counteract potential alienating effects associated with traditional shaming ("Shame, Stigma, and Crime: Evaluating the Efficacy of Shaming Sanctions in Criminal Law" 2003).

Others believe that Braithwaite's theory is practical and testable. Increasingly, Braithwaite's theory is used to study white collar crime and explain crime rates and recidivism in a variety of cultural settings. Research findings from these studies indicate some successes associated with reintegrative shaming (Miethe, Lu, and Reese 2000; Morris and Young 2000; Morris and Maxwell 2001).

Implications of Restorative Justice for Corrections

Restorative justice techniques may make corrections processes less punitive and more treatment-oriented. The emphases on healing and reintegration are particularly important to offenders and are less prevalent in traditional corrections environments. Efforts to make offenders who re-enter society into whole, contributive, productive citizens are needed. Community justice requires that communities institute informal social control at the grassroots level. The informal social controls found in families, personal associations, nonprofit and for-profit organizations, and social organizations are viewed as more important than formal social controls such as police, courts, and correctional enforcement (Clear et al. 2003, 77).

For many offenders who would like to reintegrate, community support is essential but coordination through community-based correctional structures is required to make the transition successful. Restorative justice has the potential to transform corrections with community-based input and support. Initial evaluations of restorative correctional techniques indicate that alternative community-based sanctions can have a positive impact on offenders, victims and communities.

References

Arrigo, Bruce A., and Robert C. Schehr. 1998. "Restoring Justice for Juveniles: A Critical Analysis of Victim-Offender Mediation." *Justice Quarterly* 15 (4): 629–666.

Austin, James. 2001."Prisoner Reentry: Current Trends, Practices, and Issues." *Crime and Delinquency* 47 (July): 314–334.

Book, Aaron S. 1999. "Note: Shame on You: An Analysis of Modern Shame Punishment as an Alternative to Incarceration." *William and Mary Law Review* 40: 653.

Braithwaite, John. 1989. *Crime, Shame and Reintegration*. Cambridge: Cambridge University Press.

Braithwaite, John. 2000. "Shame and Criminal Justice." *Canadian Journal of Criminology* 42 (July): 281–298.

Braithwaite, John. 2002. *Restorative Justice and Responsive Regulation*. Oxford: Oxford University Press.

Braswell, Michael, John Fuller, and Bo Lozoff. 2001. *Corrections, Peacemaking, and Restorative Justice: Transforming Individuals and Institutions*. Cincinnati: Anderson Publishing.

Bright, Christopher. "Victim-Offender Panels." (1997) < www.restorativejustice.org/Rj2f_victim_offender_panels.htm > (accessed May 23 2003).

Bright, Christopher. "Victim-Offender Mediation." (1997) < www.restorative justice.org/Rj2f_victim_offender_panels.htm > (accessed May 23 2003).

"Broken Windows" Probation: The Next Step in Fighting Crime." 1999. *Alternatives to Incarceration* 5 (September/October): 6, 10–14.

Clear, Todd R., and Eric Cadora, with Sarah Bryer and Charles Swartz. 2003. *Community Justice*. Belmont, CA: Wadsworth/Thomson Learning.

Clear, Todd R., Dina R. Rose, and Judith A. Ryder. 2001. "Incarceration and the Community: The Problem of Removing and Returning Offenders." *Crime and Delinquency* 47 (July): 335–351.

Coates, Robert B., and John Gehm. 1985. *Victim Meets Offender: An Evaluation of Victim-Offender Reconciliation Programs*. Valparaiso, IN: PACT Institution of Justice.

Coates, Robert B., Mark Umbreit, and Betty Vos. 2000. "Restorative Justice Circles in South Saint Paul, Minnesota." St. Paul, MN: Center for Restorative Justice & Peacemaking.

Cunha, Jennifer Michele. 1999. "Comment: Family Group Conferences: Healing the Wounds of Juvenile Property Crime in New Zealand and the United States." *Emory International Law Review* 13 (Spring): 283–343.

Davis, Robert, and Tonya Bannister. 1995. "Improving the Collection of Court-Ordered Restitution." *Judicature* 79:30–33.

Dean-Myrda, Mark C., and Francis T. Cullen. 1998. "The Panacea Pendulum: An Account of Community as a Response to Crime." In *Community Corrections*. Ed. Joan Petersilia. New York: Oxford University Press, pp. 3–18.

"Development in Law: Alternatives to Incarceration." 1998. *Harvard Law Review* 111 (May): 1967–1990.

Duguid, Stephen. 2000. *Can Prisons Work? The Prisoner as Object and Subject in Modern Corrections*. Toronto: University of Toronto Press.

Dzur, Albert W., and Alan Wertheimer. 2002. "Forgiveness and Public Deliberation: The Practice of Restorative Justice." *Criminal Justice Ethics* 21 (Winter): 3–20.

Etter, Gregg W., and Judy Hammond. 2001. "Community Service Work as Part of Offender Rehabilitation." *Corrections Today* 63 (December): 114–115+.

Etzioni, Amitai. 1999. "Back to the Pillory?" *The American Scholar* 68 (Summer): 43–50.

Finn, Mary A., and Suzanne Muirhead-Steves. 2002. "The Effectiveness of Electronic Monitoring With Violent Male Parolees." *Justice Quarterly* 19 (June): 293+.

Hansen, Mark. 1997. "Repairing the Damage: Citizen Boards Tailor Sentences to Fit the Crimes in Vermont." *American Bar Association Journal* 83 (September): 20.

Hay, Carter. 2001. "An Exploratory test of Braithwaite's Reintegrative Shaming Theory." *Journal of Research in Crime and Delinquency* 38 (May): 132–153.

Hines, David. 2000. *The Woodbury Police Department Restorative Justice Program Recidivism Study*. Woodbury, MN: Inter-faith Ministries.

Hughes, Patricia, and Mary Jane Mossman. 2002. "Re-Thinking Access to Criminal Justice in Canada: A Critical Review of Needs and Responses." *Windsor Review of Legal and Social Issues* 13 (March): 1–131.

Johnstone, Gerry. 2002. *Restorative Justice: Ideas, Values, Debates*. Portland, OR: Willan Publishing.

Jones, Justin. 2003. "Probation and Parole: The Savior of Corrections." *Corrections Today* 65 (February): 34–36.

Kahan, Dan M. 1996. "What Do Alternative Sanctions Mean?" *University of Chicago Law Review* 63 (Spring): 591–652.

Karp, David R. 2002. "The Offender/Community Encounter: Stakeholder Involvement in the Vermont Community Reparative Boards." In *What Is Community Justice: Case Studies of Restorative Justice and Community Supervision*. Eds. David R. Karp and Todd R. Clear. Thousand Oaks, CA: Sage Publications, pp. 61–86.

"Keeping Track of Electronic Monitoring." 1999. *Alternatives to Incarceration* 5 (November/December): 16–20.

Kleiman, Mark A.R. 1999. "Community Corrections as the Front Line in Crime Control." *UCLA Law Review* 46 (August): 1909–1925.

Kurki, Leena. 2000. "Restorative and Community Justice in the United States." *Crime and Justice* 27: 235–291.

Leaf, Robin, Arthur Lurigio, and Nancy Martin. 1998. "Chicago's Project Safeway: Strengthening Probation's Links with the Community." In *Community Corrections: Probation, Parole, and Intermediate Sanctions*. Ed. Joan Petersilia. New York: Oxford University Press, pp. 166–170.

Lucas, Nancy. 2001. "Note: Restitution, Rehabilitation, Prevention, and Transformation: Victim-Offender Mediation for First-Time Non-Violent Youthful Offenders." *Hofstra Law Review* 29 (Summer): 1365–1400.

MacKenzie, Doris Layton, Katharine Browning, Stacy B. Skroban, and Douglas A. Smith. 1999. "The Impact of Probation on the Criminal

Activities of Offenders." *Journal of Research in Crime and Delinquency* 36 (November): 423–453.

Martin, Ginger. 2003. "The Effectiveness of Community-Based Sanctions in Reducing Recidivism." *Corrections Today* 65 (February): 26–29.

Massaro, Toni M. 1991. "Shame, Culture, and American Criminal Law." *Michigan Law Review* 89 (June): 1880–1944.

Massaro, Toni M. 1997. "The Meanings of Shame: Implications for Legal Reform." *Psychology, Public Policy and Law* 3 (December): 645–703.

Mays, G. Larry, and L. Thomas Winfree, Jr. 2002. *Contemporary Corrections*. Belmont, CA: Wadsworth/Thomson Learning.

McCarney, Willie. 2001. "Responding to Juvenile Delinquency: Restorative Justice: An International Approach." *Journal of the Center for Children and the Courts* 3: 3–17.

McCarthy, Belinda Rodgers, and Bernard I. McCarthy, Jr. 1997. *Community-Based Corrections*. 3d ed. Belmont, CA: Wadsworth Publishing Co.

McDonald, John M., and David B. Moore. 2001. "Community Conferencing as a Special Case of Conflict Transformation." In *Restorative Justice and Civil Society*. Eds. Heather Strang and John Braithwaite. Cambridge: Cambridge University Press, pp. 130–148.

McMurry, Kelly. 1997. "For Shame: Paying for Crime Without Serving Time, But With a Dose of Humility." *Trial* 33 (May): 12–14.

Miethe, Terence D., Hong Lu, and Erin Reese. 2000. "Reintegrative Shaming and Recidivism Risks in Drug Court: Explanations for Some Unexpected Findings." *Crime and Delinquency* 46 (October): 522–541.

Morris, Allison, and Gabrielle Maxwell. 2001. "Restorative Conferencing." In *Restorative Justice Community: Repairing Harm and Transforming Communities*. Eds. Gordon Bazemore and Mara Schiff. Cincinnati: Anderson Publishing, pp. 173–197.

Morris, Allison, and Warren Young. 2000. "Reforming Criminal Justice: The Potential of Restorative Justice." In *Restorative Justice: Philosophy to Practice*. Eds. Heather Strang and John Braithwaite. Burlington, VT: Ashgate Publishing Co, pp. 11–31.

"Offender Supervision with Electronic Monitoring." 2003. *Corrections Forum* 12 (March/April): 70–74.

Paye, Amanda L. 1999. "Comment: Communities Take Control of Crime: Incorporating the Conferencing Model into the United States Juvenile Justice System." *Pacific Rim Law and Policy Journal* 8 (January): 161–87.

Petersilia, Joan. 2001. "Prisoner Reentry: Public Safety and Reintegration Challenges." *The Prison Journal* 81 (September): 360–375.

Phelan, Lisa C. 1997. "Note and Comment: Making Prisons Work." *Loyola of Los Angeles Law Review* 30 (June): 1789–1822.

Roach, Kent. 2000. "Changing Punishment at the Turn of the Century: Restorative Justice on the Rise." *Canadian Journal of Criminology* 42 (July): 249–280.

Rottman, David and Pamela Casey. 2000. "Therapeutic Jurisprudence and the Emergence of Problem-Solving Courts." *Alternatives to Incarceration* 6 (Spring): 27–30.

"Shame, Stigma, and Crime: Evaluating the Efficacy of Shaming Sanctions in Criminal Law." 2003. *Harvard Law Review* 116 (May): 2186–2207.

Shatzkin, Kate. 1998. "Shaming Sentences Grab Attention." *The Times-Picayune* [New Orleans] (April 26), A 20.

Skorackyj, Olga. 2000. "Work Release Programs help Inmates Succeed." *Sheriff* 52 (July/August): 22, 24.

Smith, Michael E. June 2001. "What Future for "Public Safety" and "Restorative Justice" in Community Corrections?" Washington, D.C.: U.S. Department of Justice, National Institute of Justice/ Congressional Information Service, Inc., Policy Papers.

Surkiewicz, Joe. 2002. "Maryland Instituting "Restorative Justice" Programs." *The Daily Record* [Baltimore] (April 20).

Taylor, Susan C. 1996. "Alternative Dispute Resolution Symposium: Victim-Offender Reconciliation Program—A New Paradigm Toward Justice." *University of Memphis Law Review* 26 (Spring): 1187–1195.

"The Importance of Restitution." 2000. *Corrections Forum* 9 (September/ October): 20–23.

Tonry, Michael. 1998a. "Evaluating Intermediate Sanctions." In *Community Corrections: Probation, Parole, and Intermediate Sanctions*. Ed. Joan Petersilia. New York: Oxford University Press, pp. 79–96.

Tonry, Michael. 1998b. "Intermediate Sanctions." In *The Handbook of Crime and Punishment*. Ed. Michael Tonry. New York: Oxford University Press, pp. 683–711.

Travis, Jeremy. 2001. "Reentry Reconsidered: A New Look at an Old Question." *Crime and Delinquency* 47 (July): 291–313.

Turner, Susan, and Joan Petersilia. 1996. "Work Release in Washington: Effects on Recidivism and Corrections Costs." *The Prison Journal* 76 (June): 138–164.

Turner, Susan, and Joan Petersilia. 1998. "Work Release: Recidivism and Corrections Costs in Washington State." *Alternatives to Incarceration* 4 (January/February): 10.

Turpin, James. 1999. "Restorative Justice Challenges Corrections." *Corrections Today* 61 (October): 60.

Ulrich, Gretchen. 1999. "Current Public Law and Policy Issues: Widening the Circle: Adapting Traditional Indian Dispute Resolution Methods to Implement Alternative Dispute Resolution and Restorative Justice in Modern Communities." *Hamline Journal of Public Law and Policy* 20 (Spring): 419–452.

Umbreit, Mark S. 1994. *Victim Meets Offender: The Impact of Restorative Justice and Mediation.* Monsey, NY: Criminal Justice Press.

Umbreit, Mark S., Robert B. Coates, and Betty Vos. 2002. "The Impact of Restorative Justice Conferencing: A Review of 63 Empirical Studies in 5 Countries." St. Paul, MN: Center for Restorative Justice & Peacemaking.

Van Ness, Daniel W., and Karen Heetderks Strong. 2002. *Restoring Justice.* 2d ed. Cincinnati: Anderson Publishing.

Viano, Emillo C. 2000. "Restorative Justice for Victim Offenders: A Return to American Traditions." *Corrections Today* 62 (July): 132–135.

Wachtel, Ted, and Paul McCold. 2001. "Restorative Justice in Everyday Life." In *Restorative Justice and Civil Society.* Eds. Heather Strang and John Braithwaite. Cambridge: Cambridge University Press, pp. 114–129.

Waters, Kathy L. 2003. "Probation, Parole and Community Corrections: A Difficult Topic to Understand?" *Corrections Today* 65 (February): 10.

CHAPTER 7

Conclusions

Restorative justice practices emerged in response to perceptions that the traditional criminal justice system failed on two major fronts. Zehr (2002, 21) discusses the failures associated with the traditional justice system from a restorative justice perspective. First, restorative justice advocates claim that the punishment structure utilized in the traditional criminal justice system, with its focus on doling out just deserts, generally does not prevent future crime or allow for effective reintegration of offenders into society. Second, advocates of restorative justice argue that the traditional criminal justice system does not adequately redress the damages inflicted on communities and victims by crime. Increasingly, victims, offenders, and community members feel that the traditional criminal justice system does not meet their needs. Similarly, judges, defense attorneys, prosecutors, and correctional officials also express dissatisfaction with the status quo. Some have turned to restorative justice practices as a means of addressing victim needs, repairing the harm to the community, holding offenders accountable for their actions, and involving the community in an effort to make things right.

The emphases of restorative justice differ dramatically from those of the traditional criminal justice system. Restorative justice theory views crime as a community problems and stresses the need for community involvement and empowerment in addressing the harms associated with crime. Although reducing recidivism is not the sole focus of restorative justice, advocates of restorative justice emphasize that community involvement and citizen participation in amerliorating the root causes of crime and facilitating offender reintegration will help reduce crime (Kurki 2000, 237).

From a restorative justice viewpoint, crime is more than a violation of law and an affront to State power; it represents damaged relationships. Harm to one member of the community represents harm to every member of the community. To repair this harm and make things right becomes an obligation of everyone in the community (Zehr 2002, 22). Use of restorative justice techniques creates obligations for the offender and the affronted in the community to heal and promote peace. Even when no offender has been successfully identified and apprehended, the community has a responsibility to address the needs of victims and repair the harm as much as possible (Zehr 2002, 23).

In practice, as in theory, defendants are not automatically eligible to participate in restorative justice programs. Many of these programs screen offenders for suitability and for their willingness to admit guilt and submit to a restoration plan. Concerns exist that use of restorative justice will expand the net of social control, drawing more offenders under community and judicial control than the current practices used by the traditional criminal justice system (Braithwaite 1999, 26). Evidence indicates, however, that, if net widening occurs, it will place more offenders under community control rather than State control. Preliminary evidence also suggests that offenders who participate in restorative justice programs are restored to the extent that they forego further criminal conduct (Braithwaite 1999, 27).

Victims have responded positively to restorative justice initiatives, feeling empowered to a degree that is not possible under the traditional justice system. The most widely-used program, Victim-offender mediation (VOM), receives high satisfaction ratings from victims. Victims are less likely to fear being victimized again when they participate in VOM, an indicator that inner peace has been re-established (Bazemore and Umbreit, 2001). Many victims' rights advocates embrace restorative justice practices and believe they provide a forum for victim empowerment and participation in the administration of justice.

Greater numbers of members of the courtroom workgroup—police, prosecutors, defense attorneys, and judges—have begun to seek alternatives to the adversarial nature of full-scale due process proceedings. Some are experimenting with restorative justice practices as they have become more attracted to problem-solving based on collaborative relationships. The use of whole client representation by some defense attorneys involves counseling clients to admit guilt when having their day in court could lead to punitive sentencing. Beyond this, the defense attorney helps the client obtain appropriate sentencing alternatives and make contacts with social workers, treatment centers, and community supporters in a way that facilitates successful reintegration into society (Clarke 2001). Police, through community policing and family group conferencing, are building community relationships that make them aware of community needs and make resolution of conflict and healing possible (McCold and Wachtel 1998). Prosecutors, too, use pretrial diversion as a means of putting offenders in touch with such restorative justice practices as victim restitution and victim offender reconciliation. These practices seek to reconcile the needs of the victim, the community, and the offender in order to remedy harms rather than inflict the harshest punishment possible (Gay 2000, 1652). Numerous judges have been leading the restorative justice movement as advocates of community courts and problem-solving courts, such as drug courts. Based on the recognition that courts cannot operate in a vacuum nor isolate themselves from social problems such as substance abuse or mental illness, judges have created problem-solving courts that bring community resources together on behalf of defendants and seek to look at individual and community needs in the adjudication process (Rottman and Casey 2000).

Thousands of communities have embraced use of restorative justice practices. Community involvement is of central importance in the successful implementation of restorative justice processes. Without community support and active involvement, restorative justice cannot be implemented and the harm inflicted by crime cannot be repaired. From a restorative justice viewpoint, the community as a whole is the secondary victim of crime. When it is adversely affected by crime, a community should be given the opportunity to address the issue. Restorative justice advocates argue that the closer the enforcers of norms are to offenders, the more likely they will be able to bring about desired change in their behavior. Theoretically, the community should be more effective in maintaining social control than the formal criminal justice system (Clear et al. 2003).

Used for correctional purposes, restorative justice may make punishment less punitive and more treatment oriented although critics claim that communities, bent on revenge, could be even more punitive in punishment than the traditional justice system. If restorative justice values prevail, however, the emphases on healing and reintegration are particularly important to offenders and are more likely to promote successful re-entry into society (Clear et al. 2003, 77).

Implications of Restorative Justice

Restorative justice practices can provide alternative or diversionary programs that reduce the pressure on the traditional justice system and also result in a more humane resolution to conflict and harm caused by crime (Zehr 2002, 52). Prosecutors and judges may refer a case to a restorative justice program which can tailor the sentence (or restoration plan) to fit the needs of victims, offenders, and the communities. In addition, restorative justice programs may promote healing and restoration (Zehr 2002, 52–53). Victim-offender mediation, reconciliation programs, and victim-impact panels provide forums that can have profound impacts both on victims and offenders, as well as their supporters in the community. With careful screening and preparation, these programs have been largely positive for all involved and encourage offenders to understand the consequences of their actions and to take responsibility for them. A third area—offender re-entry and transition programs—provides halfway houses and access to community resources for offenders to ensure successful reintegration (Zehr 2002, 53–54). In Vermont, the reparative boards hold offenders accountable to a restitution plan and monitor their behavior over a period of time. These three approaches—diversionary programs, healing and restoration procedures, and offender re-entry programs—may augment and transform the criminal justice system to produce greater individualized justice and greater satisfaction for all stakeholders.

The Future of Restorative Justice

Much uncertainty surrounds the implementation of restorative justice programs in the United States. The popularity of punitive measures with elected officials and the desire to be "tough on crime" may impose barriers to programs that appear to be softer on crime, no matter how effective they are.

Another potential problem for many restorative justice practices is the question of whether large numbers of victims will be willing to face and possibly confront their offenders. Victims may not want to be in the same room with offenders who inflicted pain and injury on them. They may simply wish to forget the crime. Some offenders may not be able to participate in restorative justice programs in a meaningful way due to lack of remorse or mental illness.

The courtroom workgroup's attachment to the status quo may be a difficult obstacle to overcome. The political culture in the United States, for example, with its attachment to civil liberties, due process, and an adversary process, may not be the most fertile ground for restorative justice practices. Convincing police, judges, prosecutors, and defense attorneys to buy into restorative justice programs may be a daunting task. A chicken-egg problem exists because advocates cannot demonstrate the effectiveness of these programs unless they are implemented and the programs are difficult to implement unless they have a track record of success.

Another obstacle is community involvement. Can restorative justice programs sustain the level of community participation necessary for program operations? Will support from the community taper off as restorative justice practices become more commonplace?

The future of restorative justice programs will largely depend on how effective advocates are at building support for them at the grassroots level and how able they are at demonstrating the effectiveness of these bold new approaches to justice. Successful implementation will require an incremental approach as advocates illustrate how restorative justice programs can complement existing status quo arrangements.

Initial research on restorative justice programs is promising and illustrates that these programs have many benefits to offer. Fully restorative justice is probably not realistic in the near future. As Zehr (2000, 60) notes, real world justice is more like a continuum—at one end, the Western legal system with its emphasis on adversariness and due process and at the other end, restorative justice, with its emphasis on empowerment, healing and reintegration. Perhaps it is more practical to assume that both systems will be used and the traditional system will be augmented with restorative justice practices.

References

Bazemore, Gordon, and Mark Umbreit. 2001. "A Comparison of Four Restorative Conferencing Models." *Juvenile Justice Bulletin* (February) Washington, D.C.: Office of Justice Programs, Office of Juvenile Justice and Delinquency Prevention.

Braithwaite, John. 1999. "Restorative Justice: Assessing Optimistic and Pessimistic Accounts." *Crime & Justice* 25: 1–107.

Clarke, Cait. 2001. "Problem-Solving Defenders in the Community: Expanding the Conceptual and Institutional Boundaries of Providing Counsel to the Poor." *Georgetown Journal of Legal Ethics* 14 (Winter): 401–58.

Clear, Todd R., and Eric Cadora, with Sarah Bryer and Charles Swartz, 2003. *Community Justice*. Belmont, CA: Wadsworth/Thomson Learning.

Gay, Frederick W. 2000. "Restorative Justice and the Prosecutor." *Fordham Urban Law Journal* 27 (June): 1651–1662.

Kurki, Leena. 2000. "Restorative and Community Justice in the United States." *Crime & Justice* 27: 235–391.

McCold, Paul, and Benjamin Wachtel. 1998. *Restorative Policing Experiment: The Bethlehem Pennsylvania Police Family Group Conferencing Project*. Pipersville, PA: Community Service Foundation.

Rottman, David, and Pamela Casey. 2000. "Therapeutic Jurisprudence and the Emergence of Problem-Solving Courts." *Corrections Forum* 9 (March/April): 27–30.

Zehr, Howard. 2002. *The Little Book of Restorative Justice*. Intercourse, PA: Good Books.

GENERAL EDITORS
David A. Schultz & Christina DeJong

Studies in Crime and Punishment is a multidisciplinary series that publishes scholarly and teaching materials from a wide range of methodological perspectives and explores sentencing and criminology issues from a single nation or comparative perspective. Subject areas to be addressed in this series include, but will not be limited to: criminology, sentencing and incarceration, policing, law and the courts, juvenile crime, alternative sentencing methods, and criminological research methods.

For additional information about this series or for the submission of manuscripts, please contact:

> David A. Schultz
> Peter Lang Publishing
> Acquisitions Department
> 275 Seventh Avenue, 28th floor
> New York, New York 10001

To order other books in this series, please contact our Customer Service Department:
> (800) 770-LANG (within the U.S.)
> (212) 647-7706 (outside the U.S.)
> (212) 647-7707 FAX

Or browse online by series:
> www.peterlangusa.com